Ed Fowler's

Knife Talk

The Art & Science Of Knifemaking

Published by

krause
publications

700 E. State Street • Iola, WI 54990-0001
Telephone: 715/445-2214

Please call or write for our free catalog.
Our toll-free number to place an order or obtain a free catalog is 800-258-0929
or please use our regular business telephone 715-445-2214
for editorial comment and further information.

Library of Congress Catalog Number: 97-80612
ISBN: 0-87341-584-1

* Printed in the United States of America

ACKNOWLEDGMENTS

A book doesn't just happen, nor does a man. We are all a part of everyone who came our way throughout our lives. My first role models were my grandfathers who taught me the value of honest work while instilling within me a deep appreciation of nature, art, craftsmanship and of course, knives from the start of my existence. While my grandmother was the first to teach me how to use a knife, she also taught me the importance of faith and humanity.

I hated school from kindergarten on, and still get ulcers when I hear about school starting in the fall. However, I did have a few good teachers. Robert A. Kainer, DVM, taught science in my high school. When he heard that I was planning on hitting the road as a loader operator for a construction company, rather than returning back to school, he visited me. He asked me questions about the hydraulics, mechanical advantage and the nature of the component forces that make a loader work. With my ignorance apparent, he told me that if I would return to school that fall and take his physics course, I would understand these concepts and a lot more. Thanks to his sincere interest and outstanding teaching ability, I spent the next six years in school. Thanks Doc.

Paul Burke, Attorney, member of the board of the American Bladesmith Society, gentleman and friend has sent me books, encouraged my experiments and counseled me when I fell flat on my face. Another man, without whom, this would not have come together.

There have been more authors than I can remember, Edgar Rice Burroughs taught me to read with his Tarzan books. Earnest Thomas Seaton spoke of nature, Margaret Mead spoke of cultures, Lincoln of ethics and country people.

Eric Fromm gave me an understanding of the nature of man and society, Glasser an understanding of myself. Henry Thoreau continues to provide me a little sanity when all else doesn't make sense. Charles Russell, through his art and writing, gave me no other course in life than the cowboy. All of these come together to make a knifemaker. I don't know exactly why, but that is the way it was from the beginning, so somehow, it has got to add up.

Wayne Goddard encouraged my experiments, when no one else understood the frontiers that awaited us. Bruce Voyles asked me to write, Steve Shackleford worked with my spelling, grammar and artist mentality and the articles became a joy as well as inspiration for more. David Kowalski encouraged putting all of what follows together and my devoted wife, Angela, did the impossible, put it together and got me to write this when there are knives to make.

There has to be a special thanks to my family, friends, and John Strohecker, our hired hand and apprentice, who do the extra work to give me time to devote to knives and writing.

Special thanks to Bill Moran, who introduced me to the nature of the forged blades and steel.

Most of my life has been blessed with good dogs who shared time with nature and knives and me. They have pulled me out of some serious wrecks, always been there in good times and bad, their sharing making it all better.

Special thanks to the readers of Blade magazine who have encouraged me to write more, shared their thoughts with me—inspiring future articles. We all became good friends.

Thanks to my son, Matt, and who could forget Blue—as fine a dog as any man could want.

FOREWORD

There's no mistaking an Ed Fowler knife. It's a working knife that will actually work long and sharp. Most of his blades have that gradual curve to the tip that makes skinning game a pleasure or fashioning a tent stake a simple matter. And your slippery hand can't run up the blade to bloody disaster because a distinct guard protects you. Then we get to the unique sheephorn handle, rugged as the range rams that contributed to this piece of working man's art and craft.

There's no mistaking Ed Fowler. He's the same cowboy at a New York knife show as he is on his Wyoming ranch. You'll see the same white cowboy hat, the same white beard, the same twinkle in the eye that tells you he's thinking far more than he's saying.

There's no mistaking Ed Fowler's writing. A little knife lore. A little philosophy. Then some knifemaking science. Ed conveys a healthy dose of the scientist's sense of wonder at how the natural world works. He knows how knives work, why they work. And then he tells you how the artist can combine form and function in one knife to create a thing of beauty.

Henry David Thoreau, an eastern cowboy of sorts, once commented that "...the earth is soft and impressible by the feet of men." He walked a trail through the woods to his beloved Walden Pond. And he influenced a legion of admiring readers who were left with new trails through their minds after they read them.

I hope Ed Fowler gives you a new and intriguing view of the world of knives in this collection of his magazine articles. We think he'll leave a positive impression in your mind of the art and science of knifemaking.

David D. Kowalski
Publisher
BLADE Magazine

This work is dedicated to my granddaughter,
Kassie Jo
who left us way too soon.

INTRODUCTION

I have made knives off and on since the sixth grade, and I am devoted to the using knife as a tool and art form. I sometimes feel that the true using knife is in danger of extinction. Many knives that I see sold lack the functional quality they need. As a rancher, there are many times that a good functional knife can mean the difference between life and death.

Don't get me wrong, I realize that not everyone wants or needs a high performance knife. I don't expect everyone to agree with me concerning the functional attributes of a knife. I do feel very strongly that knife function is poorly understood by many people. Therefore, many of my ideas revolve around my concepts about the truly "functional" knife of my dreams.

The following pages contain technical information for the knife maker, hopefully written in a language all can understand. More importantly, they speak of people with smiles and tears and dreams. I imply a challenge to all who would come to the world of knives, for whatever reason, to join a fraternity of people as diverse as any, and honest as they come. Share your talents, explore the frontiers that await you and most importantly, know you are welcome.

CONTENTS

CHAPTER 1

Function, Design, & Techniques

I was new at writing, "Can Your Knife Cut It?", had a lot of information in one article. I was walking on cloud nine, expecting a revolution in the world of knives, handles that fit and were comfortable, guards that protected hands and didn't bite your hand would be the rule rather than the exception. I knew that practical sheaths would be on knives everywhere. It took some months and my optimism slowly melted as I realized that when you put too much information in one place, only a small part of it sticks. With a few exceptions, each person that I talked to about the article only remembered one aspect. From that time on each article I wrote would speak only to one message, emphasized several times in as many ways as I could figure out to put it. High performance knives can be made that are safe, practical and user friendly, it all starts with design. While an entire book could easily be written on the design of a truly functional knife, in my opinion the following thoughts are a start down the trail to good times with a knife.

Knife shown is "Prong Horn" 4-3/4 inch blade, sheep horn handle.

Can Your Knife Cut It?

Introduction

I have tried to carry about every knife design that had any hope of practicality. Knives, like people, are best when doing the job they were designed for. Some designs are specialists. Skinners, for example, are great for skinning, but due to the curve in the blade can lack dexterity and may actually be dangerous when you try to accomplish other tasks with them. No single blade design can do it all with the greatest degree of efficiency, and a man can only carry one knife on his belt comfortably. Therefore, a knife that is going to be your primary tool must be a compromise fitted up for the work you do. At the time of this book, I believe that the design I call the "Pronghorn" has proven itself to be my favorite. The "Pronghorn" design can get me through any chore I have to do considering safety, efficiency and comfort. The point is thin enough to dig in to your work when necessary and the belly is adequate for skinning. For my kind of work I like the blade heavy enough to chop and pry when necessary, giving up a little cutting efficiency in order to gain strength as a heavy duty blade will not slice as well as a thin one. If I raised frogs instead of cows, and lived in the city rather than a ranch, the knife I carried would probably look like this one, but be scaled down considerably.

Most knives are designed with a range of functions in mind; these can include anything from hanging on a wall to skinning a moose. Many hunters like to carry the smallest knife possible while in the field. Most North American game can be field dressed with a one-inch blade. While far from ideal, field dressing most game with a one-inch blade is possible.

Now let's change the rules of the game, as fate can do so easily. Imagine you are hunting deer, carrying a three-inch blade and a sudden turn of a log breaks your leg. You are miles from camp. The gathering clouds are now releasing huge wet flakes of snow. You sit wondering what to do, and come to the conclusion that the handy little blade would be much better if it was now a 12 inch blade. A blade large enough to chop firewood, cut a splint, and to aid in building a shelter.

When selecting a knife I feel that you should take as many consequences into consideration as possible. The 12 inch blade is probably out of the question as it is heavy and cumbersome, and would probably be left in camp. I like to carry a knife that is designed to accomplish routine tasks, heavy enough to use under exigent circumstances, but still comfortable and handy to carry so that one has it with him when necessary.

To be useful, a knife must be instantly available for use. This is most especially true in life or death situations. For example, a rancher uses rope constantly, both from horseback and on foot. Rope is often used when administering medication to beef cattle. A cow can choke down on a rope which is tied to a tree or post, likely as not falling back as she goes down, leaving up to 1,200 pounds tension on the rope. I hate to cut a $20 rope, but when the choice is between a $20 rope and a $400 cow, the cow wins every time. Usually, you can untie the rope but occasionally you have to cut the rope and cut it fast.

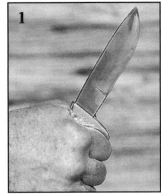

(Above) (1) The guard keeps the hand from slipping up the blade, and the smooth blade back is easy on the user's thumb when force is needed during cutting. (2) The Ricasso allows the user to choke the knife for added leverage while still having full use of the guard. 3) For detail work, move the hand to within an inch of the blade tip. The Ricasso and full guard are handy for such work. 4) The full, rounded handle butt enables the user to drive the tip of the knife into an object using nothing more than the palm of the hand as the driving force. such "splitting action" is invaluable in field use and is not hard on the knife or user if the knife is designed properly.

(top) The author's second completed Damascus blade, 312 layers of 5160 and mild steels. (middle) Ed's first wire cable Damascus blade. (bottom) Fowler's sheep foot design. The author has used these designs to butcher countless animals and "cut everything I needed to cut in the field." Full guards, smooth backs and 3/4-inch Ricassos make these knives easy and safe to use, according to Ed. (Fowler photo)

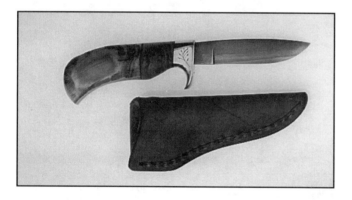

The scabbard Ed carries. He feels that, "Fourteen ounce waxed harness leather is very durable and does not rust a blade the way other treatments of leather can." (Fowler photo)

I have seen cowboys caught up in a tangled rope or stirrup, being dragged across the ground or accidentally tied to a recalcitrant cow who was intent on making mush out of a man. I could easily relay dozens more of these situations. Usually they result from inexperience, carelessness or haste. The fact is accidents happen. Many times a rancher is alone and must depend on his own ability and preparedness to come out of the situation favorably.

When time is short, and yet you must retrieve the knife from the scabbard or unfold it, your knife needs to be ready instantly for action. This dictates that the knife must be a fixed blade which can be removed from a sheath with one hand and be ready to cut. The scabbard on my using knife is a pouch type, similar to the type carried by frontiersmen.

To aid the removal of the knife from the scabbard, I prefer a swell and hook at the butt end of the knife handle. This allows a positive grip and the knife can easily be removed from the scabbard even while engaged in what can best be described as exciting circumstances. Not only must the knife be available, it must be designed to provide maximum safety for the user. This means when your body is full of adrenaline, or you are in the process of being stomped by a frightened or aggravated animal, you can grab the knife, remove it from the scabbard, cut rope or leather with little chance of your hand slipping forward from the handle to slice your fingers on the blade.

Years ago, this happened to one of my friends who had shot an exceptional bull elk after a long stalk. He had wounded the bull and spent some time tracking him down. After killing the bull he was both fatigued and excited. While he was reaching into the elk's body cavity to sever the dia-

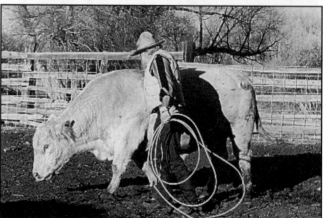

Animals and rope go together—sometimes you can get into a wreck and a readily handy knife can make a difference. While I have only had to cut a rope fast four times in thirty-five years, carrying the knife was well worth it.

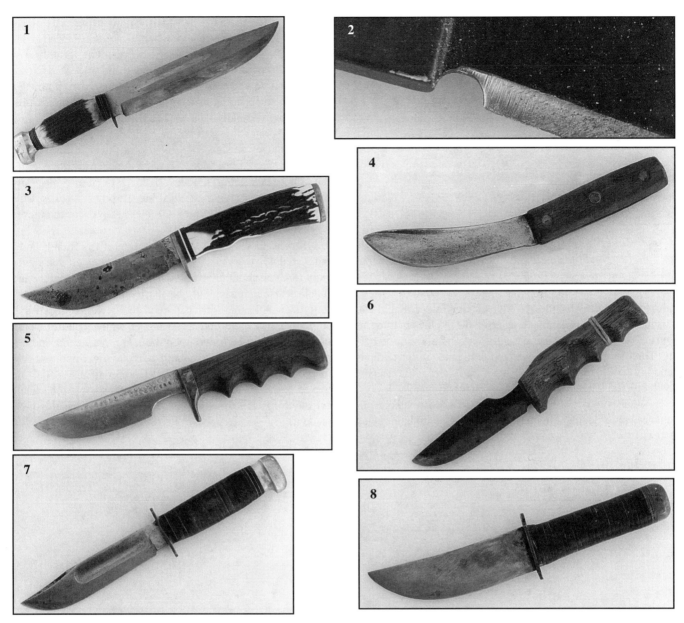

(Note: The author uses these knives to illustrate knife features he disapproves of, not to ridicule any particular maker - Ed.) (1) A big camp knife the midline bevel on the blade reduces cutting efficiency, the fullers serve no purpose, and the guard is too flimsey, sharp and uncomfortable. Its Ricasso is too short for any functional advantage, and the knife will hang up where the edge drops from the Ricasso. (2) I personally consider a "nick" on the blade where the edge meets the Ricasso a serious design fault when a functional field knife is the goal. (3) I feel the tip on this is too high and pointy, the swell on the spine (top) of the blade serves no functional purpose, the guard is sharp and uncomfortable and the flat butt of the handle would be better if it were rounded. (4) This is an old knife purchased at the estate auction of a Wyoming pioneer family. Its well used design dictates it's a specialist, a skinner. This kind of knife is fairly safe when used as a skinner, but can be dangerous when used for field use, other than skinning. It's best kept in your saddlebags, pickup, or left in camp. (5) One of my early creations—the deep finger grooves limit the knives utility to one grip, the deep choil will hang up when you try to use it.(6) Another of my early knives—the thumb notch on the spine quickly wears on my thumb. While useful as a file, it is a poor knife due to the cutting resistance of the file teeth on the blades sides when cutting flesh. (7) This is the first sheath knife I ever purchased. I used it for years—the fullers on the blade's sides got me in trouble on several occasions when they hung up cutting a sternum from ribs and splitting a pelvis. The choil hung up many times in skinning hide, and the guard wasn't friendly to my hand. (8) My first completed knife. The guard is too sharp, unfriendly to my hand and interferes with function. Blade too much curve-spine too straight. (Fowler photos)

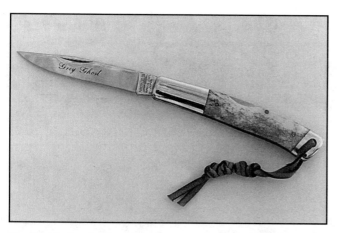

Parker Cutlery's Grey Ghost—my favorite pocket knife blade design. It's good for digging out splinters, lancing abscesses on cows, and delicate work.

phragm from the ribs, the tip of his locking folder caught and his hand slid across the blade severing the tendons in two fingers. That ended the hunting trip for him and his hunting party. Three hours of surgery were required to repair the tendons and his hand was stiff and the finger that was cut the deepest and took the longest to heal was his trigger finger.

Whenever you are excited, fatigued or distracted, your chances of an accident increase. I feel a full guard helps stack the odds a little more in your favor. On my using knife I have a guard which extends from the handle a full 7/8 inch (inside radius). The guard is curved to fit my finger comfortably. The sides and front of the guard are rounded and smoothed to provide a flexible and comfortable grip. At first, a guard of this size tends to get in your way; however, with practice a full-curved guard actually increases control of the blade.

I also prefer at least a 5/8-inch smooth Ricasso in front of the guard. This permits placement of a finger in front of the guard on a smooth surface, allowing the user to choke up on the knife when doing delicate skinning. I can also place my thumb forward on the blade's spine for power strokes. This reduces fatigue, in that you no longer have a four inch lever working against your wrist.

I recall that several years ago, eight of my friends and I butchered 49 steers in 19 hours. I learned then all that I ever want to know about fatigue and using knives. Both safety and function also dictate a knife be sharp only on the desired cutting edge. All other surfaces need to be well rounded and smoothed. File nicks and sharp angles, while beautiful works of art, are not to be found upon the knife that I carry and depend. Additionally, the scabbard also plays an important role in providing safety for the user. I prefer to use 12-14 oz. waxed harness leather. I have carried one such scabbard every day for five years and it is still as functional as the day I made it.

To Have And To Hold

Carefully examine the human hand and try to find a straight line in it. You won't. Everything is rounded; smooth, gentle curves of flesh, muscle and bone flow from one to another. It follows, then, that the knife handle must have the polished, graceful curves and forms of nature to caress the hand that will carry it.

Feel the contours of your hand muscles. Flex your hand. Work your fingers and thumb like you're working a piece of clay and note how versatile your hand is at conforming to the many shapes it is required to handle. From holding a telephone to the steering wheel of your car, from gripping a pencil to the door knob of your house, your hands are what makes the world around you work. The adaptability of your hands is the key to your working world. The handle is where the knife and man meet. Every hand is as special and individual as the person to whom it belongs.

Factory vs. Handmade Grips

It is an economic necessity that most, if not all, factory or mass-produced blades have universal handles. Should any large knife manufacturer attempt to provide custom handles on a major product line, it could easily find itself in a logistical nightmare. While not perfect for all people, many of the universal handles the factories provide get the job done for most blade users.

The handmade knife is where the man who wants a handle that speaks to his hand with kindness and uncompromised function can easily realize his dream. There are custom handles that fit your hand as naturally as your favorite old gloves. When using the custom handle, it should match your hand so well you are scarcely aware of it. I read one time that all knife handles should be symmetrical. The only trouble with that is I have never seen or felt a symmetrical hand. Symmetrical grips are for mass-produced blades and for people who don't understand the dynamics of the human hand. Right-handed handles for right-handed people and left-handed grips for southpaws are both possible and practical goals for the knifemaker and blade lover to seek.

There are times when custom handles are designed with art, rather than function, in mind. These handles usually have sharp edges and curves that bring new meaning to the terms pain, discomfort and carpal tunnel syndrome. When you see and feel such grips, accept them for what they are: art. There is nothing wrong with art handles. They bring joy to many makers and knife lovers. While such grips may be visually pleasing, they aren't meant to excel as a using tool.

Though it's possible to make a handle that feels pretty good to all who will use it, any grip that fits all hands is a compromise that fails to speak to the individual. While some universal handles are better than others, they are a compromise of the ideal.

J.D. Smith's graceful short sword fits J.D.'s hand like a glove and speaks well for the message of the handmade knife. Smith's address: 516 Second, Dept. BL, S. Boston, MA 02127 (617) 269-1699.

The Human Factor

One aspect of human behavior that has always amazed me is the reluctance to modify tools, no matter how poorly designed they may be. Before I started making knives, I felt that all tools were sacred. Whenever I found a tool lacking in quality or design, I merely accepted its shortcomings and worked with it.

Soon after I started making blades, I found that many of the tools I used could be better. Now, I don't hesitate when a certain task requires that I change a tool. I grind, bend, weld and, in short, do whatever it takes to make the tool more appropriate for the job at hand.

Another all-too-common fact of human nature is that most people are willing to adapt to tools that sadly lack in the area of user friendliness. Many who make a living with blades use some of the most poorly designed knives available. Due to these blades' ready availability and the adaptive qualities of the human body, such people can make the knives work for them. They accept the poorly designed handle because they don't know any better. They get used to it over time and, due to the nearly unlimited ability of the human body to adapt and use almost any poorly designed tool, the traits of the inferior design become standards that the entire cutlery industry comes to recognize as high quality. If you doubt it, look at how many knife blades have spines that shave wood, guards that cut skin and still allow the hand to slip onto the blade, and handles that limit the knives' functional characteristics.

When you seek a blade that will be put to heavy use, the handle must feel like a natural extension of the hand. At the same time, the quest for symmetrical handles is against all attributes of the hand.

The grip of Wayne Goddard's bowie allows a comfortable hand hold and caresses Wayne's hand like an old friend. This piece won best handforged knife at the 1996 Oregon Knife Show. Goddard's address: 473 Durham, Dept. Bl, Eugene, OR 97404 (541) 689-8098.

Materials & Hand Holds

A handle material cannot be slippery. Conversely, materials that offer too much friction between hand and handle will give you blisters. Years ago, I decided on a checkered knife grip. It looked good and felt good for a short time but, when it came to real cutting work, my hand felt like it had been on the wrong end of a horseshoe rasp. The same thing happened with a handle made from a new, non-skid material developed for shoe soles. The grip felt good for a while but it didn't take long before it gave me blisters. Whenever I use a knife, I constantly shift my grip. The non-skid texture of the handle pulled on my skin every time my grip shifted.

One time, when I was just getting started seriously making knives, I watched some professionals use blades on the kill floor of a local packing plant. I recorded the hand holds used on the knives for butchering beef. The result of four hours of observation was that there was no single predominant hold on the handle. The workers' hands constantly shifted position throughout, beyond the range of grips I had initially identified. The ideal knife handle must be designed to accommodate all positions in which it will be held during use.

Whenever a maker asks about handle or blade designs and materials, I suggest that he take his best design and cut something that takes a lot of work and time. Not only will the maker learn a lot about the steel he is using, he will also discover all he needs to know about curves, knives, and handle design and material, as well as how to sharpen a knife. When you learn to appreciate the laws and beauty of nature, knife handles and other works of art used in your hands will be more appropriate for their assigned tasks.

Find The Most Solid Ground For Your Blade

Ed aboard Sonny, the successor to Monk, who died this past summer. Note how the sheathed knife at Ed's side is short enough not to dig into his leg or Sonny's saddle. (Fowler photo)

I do not intend to discuss blade styles, but to instead focus attention on the various major methods of shaping or grinding blades. Specifically, I wish to discuss the flat-ground blade, the hollow-ground blade and the convex or Moran blade. Emphasis will be placed upon how these blade types relate to function in a knife that will be used in the field.

The requirements of the field-used knife should be such that your knife will perform its "primary" function. If you are hunting deer, the primary function is obvious-or is it? I spend (or used to, before I took making knives so seriously) most of my time outdoors; some of it on horseback, some on a trail bike, some on tractors or in pickups. The common denominator of all my outdoor activities is that I carry the tool I need.

Through the years the knife that I've carried has performed a wide variety of tasks, such as scraping a moldboard plow that wouldn't scour or very carefully cutting a tenderized porcupine out of a John Deer 55 combine's concave. Once I used the knife to cut a coffee can off my favorite horse's hoof. Some kids had been fishing and discarded their worm can. Months later, Monk, who was my friend and companion for over 20 years, stepped into it. I was lucky enough to find him before the can had been on his foot long enough to do any serious damage. He was over a mile from the house, and my knife was the best tool I had with me.

My knife also has done what it was supposed to: dressing and skinning animals, both domestic and wild; numerous epi-

siotomies on first-calf heifers; and even a caesarean section when necessary. The list could go on indefinitely. The point is, a knife in the field need do not only that which it is supposed to, but also what it must. When designing a knife for the outdoorsman, I like to take the possibility of exigent circumstances into consideration.

I do not mean to imply that any knife is indestructible. My knives normally "retire" earlier than you might expect due to frequent sharpening and regrinding. Some are also slightly bent. In order to be dependable under all circumstances, a knife needs be as strong and as tough as possible. When designing a using knife for the outdoorsman, I have been able to resolve some aspects of knife design fairly easily. These aspects pertain to what is commonly called the blade grind. Three basic grind designs dominate today's knives: flat-ground, hollow-ground and the convex or "Moran" edge.

1. Flat-Ground Blade

Flat-ground blades can be obtained on a milling machine, hand-filed or ground. Both blade sides are flat to the edge. The cutting edge is then ground at a certain angle, anywhere from 17 to 35 degrees. These grinds make fine blades and there are scores of them in existence. Used within reason, they get the job done. The problem with the flat-ground blade is that the cut is made with three surfaces. A second problem is that the blade is thin near the edge and can chip out when put to hard use. Flat-ground knives are relatively easy to sharpen.

2. Hollow-Ground Blade

The hollow-ground blade is a popular and widely used blade design. What is not generally known is that the first hollow-ground blades were made by a knife manufacturer and sold to slaughter houses as a cheap "disposable" knife to replace the more traditional blades supplied at the time. The manufacturer could save time and labor grinding hollow-ground blades because they were easier to sharpen. They were also money makers because they did not last as long as the more traditional blades and were discarded when no longer serviceable. They didn't last—the edges chipped out when put to heavy work and hollow-ground blades were soon abandoned for such work.

3. Convex Edge

In my opinion, the best blade on a using knife is the one having what is commonly called the convex edge. This blade was designed by top makers such as Bill Scagel and Bill Moran, the knifemaker who "rediscovered" Damascus steel and who promoted convex grinds over hollow- and flat-ground blades.

The convex edge starts on the back of the blade and gracefully flows to the edge or tip. The convex edge's most important feature is that enough steel remains above the cutting edge to provide the strength necessary in a using blade. I also believe that such blades can be made sharper than blades with the other two grinds. The reason being, that there is only one cutting edge adequately supported by the remaining blade.

The convex edge is more difficult and time consuming to build than the other two designs. However, it is well worth the extra effort. It is widely claimed that the convex edge is difficult to sharpen. Not true. I have sharpened knives with the convex type edge many times in the field, using nothing more than a smooth rock. When available, only a steel or stone is necessary to provide the average convex edge user with years of service.

The Back of The Blade

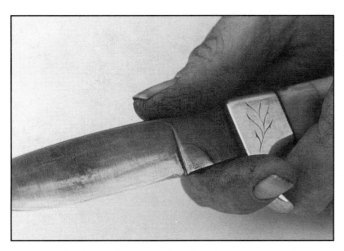

My using knife. It's been rode hard and put away wet for over a year. This is the grip I use most of the time. Placing the thumb on the spine of the blade greatly increases the knife's cutting ability.

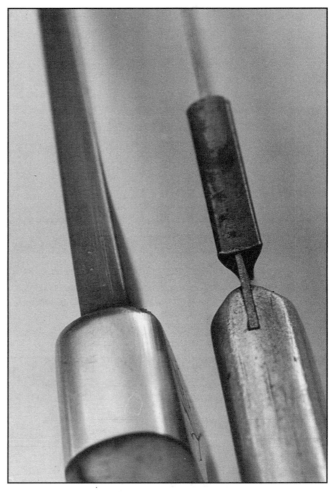

Two blades, one with a thin blade and the added spring steel clip. The other knife has a wide, smooth back. Exiting the guard it measures 114 inch thick. Tapering the blade to the tip reduces weight and the wide smooth back is user friendly.

When it comes to functional knives, the physical characteristics of the back or "spine" of the blade make the difference between a great knife and a knife that is merely better than nothing. The back of the blade serves several functions on a using knife. It can be a source of strength and comfort or a source of pain, aggravation and weakness; it is all a matter of design. A properly designed knife blade has a spine that doesn't interfere with the blade's ability to cut.

Gut hooks, saw teeth and fancy file work on the back of the blade are hazardous to your hand, detract from the practical/functional qualities of a knife, and can weaken the blade. These features cost more than they're worth. I once tried a knife with an extremely functional saw-tooth back. The combination made for a poor saw and a lousy knife. My experience with a gut-hook skinner was equally frustrating.

I like a blade spine that exits the guard or handle approximately 1/4 inch thick. A thick blade gives the knifemaker enough room to provide a smooth, rounded, cushion-like surface on which your thumb can ride when added force and control is required to cut efficiently. I prefer a thick blade that tapers to the tip. This balances the functional qualities of the knife. Thickness provides comfort and strength while taper reduces unnecessary weight without sacrificing adequate strength. Backpackers and folks who like lightweight gear may find the added weight of a thick blade detrimental. I carry a knife that weighs about 1/2 lb. Should you like a lighter blade, shorten it rather than select a thin one.

The sharp, square corners that you see and feel on too many of today's knives are nothing more than a knife that's not finished. Thick blades require extra labor and materials to finish into an efficient cutting instrument. Rounding the spine of a blade requires a little extra effort and skill from the custom knifemaker or manufacturer. Unfortunately, the blade with the sharp top lines has become so accepted that it is a mark of workmanship and quality in some circles. This is the unfortunate result of the fact that most knives are never put to the ultimate test in the field. That doesn't mean that the knife user should accept less than optimum functional quality, but that he can probably get away with less than optimum functional quality. I would rather be adequately prepared.

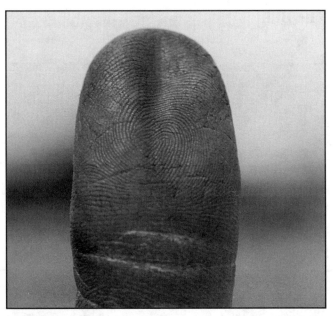

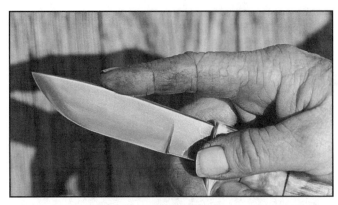

Delicate, efficient cutting is possible when the blade is friendly to your hand. When I use a knife, my hands are all over it with the exception of the cutting edge. Leverage and control make using a knife a pleasure.

(Above) My thumb after pressing into the spine of a knife with a wide/smooth rounded spine. Feels good, the pressure was distributed over a wide area, and it didn't dig into my thumb.

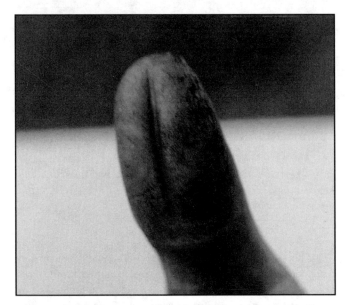

(Above) My thumb after pressing into the spine of a thin blade for the same time at the same pressure. Note the sharp, distinct impression it left on my thumb. Such knives are not user friendly.

Good Knives and Good Sheaths A Perfect Fit

Time and time again I hear people talk about the knives they have lost. In over 40 years of carrying and using knives, I have lost only one and that knife was lost for less than an hour.

In below-zero weather I was dragging a dressed mule deer down a snow-covered hillside. I slipped and fell and the buck and I tumbled for about 40 yards. Later, I noticed that my knife was missing. The scabbard was one that covered only the blade, which was held in place by a keeper strap with a snap. I had either not snapped the keeper or it came unsnapped during the fall. I returned to the hillside and found the knife, luckily, laying on top of the snow. That is the last scabbard of that type I have ever carried.

Ed added a leather-thong tie to supplement the snap on his personal scabbard. (Fowler photo)

When I started making scabbards, I carefully looked over many scabbard designs in order to determine what I consider to be the best design for a using knife. It didn't take long to decide that snaps and ties were out when outside in -30 degree weather-they were too much trouble. Such snaps and ties are too easily cut or come undone.

Rather than being returned to the scabbard, where knives belong when not in use, knives tend to be laid down and lost. I have never lost a knife out of a pouch-type scabbard. This says a lot as I carry a knife on my belt 18 hours a day, seven days a week, both afoot and on horseback. I have had the same scabbard on my belt for the past five years. Careful examination of old leather products told me that there is a place in sheaths for rivets and for stitches. My scabbards are made to last and I will replace any scabbard that the owner can wear out.

The scabbard must fit the knife snugly. This is a must, for a knife that rattles around in the scabbard is never sharp. The handle of the knife sticks out to provide an adequate grip for instant and reliable removal. For security, the guard should fit at least 1-1/2 to 2 inches into the scabbard. The rest is up to you. If you don't wish to lose your knife, you must practice replacing the knife into the scabbard until you can easily do so without looking, using your index finger as a guide. The design of the scabbard, allowing one-handed removal and placement of the knife, makes it easy. You practice and placement into a scabbard becomes a habit. Then you promise yourself that you will never lay the knife down in the field and you will probably not lose the knife.

My preference in leather has run from oak tan, to latigo and finally comes solidly to rest with waxed harness leather, anywhere from twelve to fourteen ounces. Waxed harness leather is the absolute winner for durability and ease of care. Knives stored in waxed harness leather do not have the proclivity to rust that you see in other types of leather.

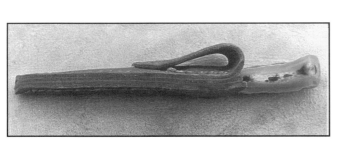

A thick welt adds stability to the scabbard, while a wide welt protects the stitching. (Fowler photo)

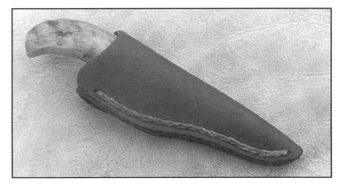

The knife slides in a good 1 1/2 inches to a snug fit in this pouch-type sheath. Ed prefers using lacing tape instead of rivets in the stitching because rivets tend to tear out due to the play in the leather at the point of attachment. (Fowler photo)

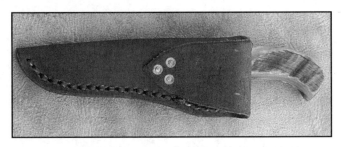

When securing the belt loop, rivets are preferable to stitching because the knife edge may cut the stitching during normal sheath use. The combination of three rivets, flat side in and hammered smooth, provides a secure and long-lasting method of attachment. (Fowler photo)

A full guard provides a surface that allows the welt to be cut so that the knife has a platform on which to rest in the scabbard, thus protecting the stitching from being cut by the knife edge. (Fowler photo)

I believe that some may like oak tan better because it is probably nicer looking, can be tooled, dyed and molded. The problem that I have with oak tan is that it must be oiled regularly or it tends to crack when subjected to water, blood and solvents.

Waxed harness leather is an oil-tanned leather, which is difficult to dye, tool or mold. It is soft, pliable, tends to repel water and is stiff enough to make a good scabbard. An occasional rubdown of "trewax" or other leather wax is all that is needed. A heavy leather welt sandwiched between the sides of the scabbard is an absolute necessity to protect stitches from being cut by the knife. I strongly prefer the rest of the scabbard to be made from one piece of leather, with the belt loop folded back and down and secured with at least three rivets. I never use rivets on the scabbard seam.

The best stitching material I have used to date is #520 waxed-nylon lacing tape made by Ludlow Industries in Ludlow, MA 01056. The longest-lasting stitch I have used is a chain-lock stitch utilizing four strands. Pulled down, it takes on a look very similar to rawhide. It is wide, lies flat and does not cut into the leather. All of my scabbards are hand stitched, most having at least 20 feet of lacing tape in them. I know of no superior method of scabbard design or construction.

If It's Not A Folder, Is It Fixed?

Don't get me wrong, I'm not prejudiced against folding knives. Some of my best friends carry one. I even have a few myself. I wouldn't want my daughter to marry a guy who relied on a folder for anything other than cleaning his fingernails or performing the light, easy kind of work for which folders were meant, but I am open minded concerning their usefulness.

Working knives need to be strong enough to serve their owners faithfully when the going gets tough. A working knife has got to be something on which you can depend. What gets folders in trouble is that too many of them are applied to situations they weren't designed to handle. They may be sold on the premise that they are up to any task they may be required to tackle. However, when it comes to actually doing the job, they too often end up quitting before the task is finished, sometimes even cutting the hand that uses them.

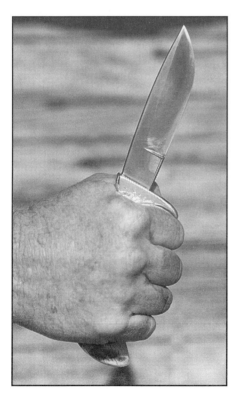

The best guard is one done properly on a fixed blade.

The First Knives

The knives that fed and clothed man from the beginning of time were fixed blades. The first of these were probably made of bone, then stone, then nonferrous metals like copper and bronze. Finally came steel. Fixed blades fed and clothed man when survival depended upon the knife he carried. The fixed blade helped him make tools, fight enemies and build shelter.

While the fixed blade helped man fight his major battles on the frontiers of survival, something new appeared-the folder. Back when life was safe and secure and there were carpeted parlors, boardrooms and bordellos, the folder was delicate, refined and pretty. The folks who carried her and relied upon her as their primary tool weren't very often in a situation where much of a knife was needed. All they required was something to trim their fingernails, cut some string or paper once in a while, or maybe whittle to pass the time. This was known as civilization.

The frontier fixed blade met the cute little bordello folder and they produced a child out of wedlock-the locking folder. It didn't have the strength or dependability of the father or cute little frame of the mother. Still, knife people have been trying to keep the lockback alive in situations where it just doesn't belong. It can't be expected to do what its dad, the fixed blade, could do in the real work place, nor can it move in the delicate, lace-curtained world of its mother. It belongs somewhere in between.

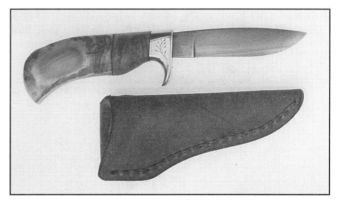

A well designed fixed blade with a well designed sheath is a hard package to beat.

Is It A Fixed-Blade World?

No folder is as strong as a well-constructed sheath knife. Anything mechanical wears out. The more you use a folder, the closer you come to the day when it will give out. When I use a knife, usually I work with a light touch. Most quality folders can stand up to this kind of use. Still, when the chips are down and you need to apply muscle to the knife, you take a chance by using a folder, a chance that can result in serious consequences.

I have never seen a folder that had anything close to an adequate guard. When the going gets tough, it may be the guard that keeps you from serious injury. Lacerated tendons are a potentially crippling injury. At best you will have a pretty hefty hospital bill and plenty of discomfort to remind you that the guard should have been there.

Don't get me wrong, there are a lot of sheath knives that also lack adequate guards. Difference is, the sheath knife doesn't limit the possibility of an adequate guard, while the folder does. It's unlikely any folder will have an adequate or comfortable guard.

Folders have another fault that is especially aggravating in the field, namely, they're a hassle to clean. Get one wet in below-zero weather and it can freeze up. Put one away with blood on it and it can seize up. It is one thing to clean a folder in the comfort of your kitchen with all kinds of brushes handy, as well as lots of hot water and an oil can on the shelf. It is another story when you are in the boondocks dressing out a bull elk in the snow and the temperature is well below freezing.

The Safety Factor

I often hear that a folder is safer to carry than a sheath knife because the folder is carried closed with the blade safely tucked into the handle. Sure it is potentially safer when it is not being used, but it is also harder to get into action when you need it in a hurry.

Years ago we had a hired hand who carried a lockback. He spent more time getting it open, closing it and putting it away than he spent using it. During the winter, it took him several minutes to get the folder to operate through all the heavy clothing he wore.

Most of the time it takes two hands to get a folder into action. When it is cold outside you have more trouble, especially when you are wearing gloves or, worse yet, mittens. Putting the knife away is also tasking because it takes two hands and you are more likely to lay it down for an instant rather than close it, only to discover hours later that you forgot to pick it back up.

There are a lot of sheath knives carried in sheaths in which I put little trust. A poorly designed sheath can be hazardous to your health. A well-designed sheath knife, paired with a well-designed sheath, is by far the best choice when you want a knife on which you can depend when the chips are down. It would be a different story if you could plan when you'll need the extra margin of performance from a well-designed sheath knife. Trouble is, you can't plan when circumstances will spring their surprises on you.

Conclusion

Any knife is better than no knife at all. The man using it has to understand its limitations. There may come a day when knives are rated for toughness. A five-star knife would be up to any task, while a one-star knife would be limited to grandmother's sewing basket. There is nothing wrong with light-duty, pretty knives. They just need to be understood and used within their limitations.

Best Military Knife Design Of All?

For the first 15 years of my life, whenever I looked at military blades, I believed that the people who designed them knew a whole lot more about knives than I did. I read how certain blades were superior combat tools, watched them being used in the movies and immediately bought one or more of the knives, only to find that I was unable to make them work. I devoted many hours working them on a wet stone trying to sharpen them. The knives' cutting ability improved somewhat but they still performed poorly. I reground them and reshaped the blades, and sometimes came up with something that was a little bit better than nothing. Some of the blades were too hard, though most were too soft.

I got to feeling pretty bashful about my ability with knives. There had to be something wrong with me because the government wouldn't supply our fighting men with junk-everybody knew that! It took time but I finally concluded that the men who designed knives' for the military, the men who purchased knives for the military and the men who made knives for the military were not all primarily concerned with making the best tool for the job. Some of them may have thought they were providing the best knife for the job, they just didn't know any better. Others were more concerned with profit or their egos. Every now and then I come across an exception to the all-too-often-seen bureaucratic monuments to stupidity. One of the nicest knives I have seen among the hundreds of military pieces is the Western Parachutist Knife No. W31.

Blade Show Find

At the 1995 Blade Show and International Cutlery Fair in Atlanta, Georgia, I was taking some time away from my table to look over the thousands of knives at the world's largest knife show. I came to the table of Larry Thomas, a well-known and respected dealer in fine knives, and curator of the American Military Edged Weaponry Museum in Intercourse, Pennsylvania. On his table was the finest example of a Western Parachutist Knife I have ever handled. I had seen photos of the knife and always liked it, but holding it confirmed beyond a doubt that it is one of the all-time greats when it comes to military blades.

The blade measures 4-3/16 inches long, 15/16 inch wide, and 3/32 inch thick. The knife is 8-5/8 inches long overall.

The butt and guard are aluminum and the handle is cocobolo sandwiched between black fiber spacers.

According to *Levine's Guide to Knives and Their Values*, the knife was made in two variations: one with a single-edge, fullered blade, the other with a double-edge, plain blade. According to Bernard Levine, the book's author, the double-edge version was never adopted and, in my opinion, would not have been as good a knife as the single-edge version.

A noteworthy feature of the parachutist knife is that the fuller (also known as the blood groove) is not very prominent. Fullers originally were designed to reduce the knife's weight. Some argue that fullered pieces may be stronger due to the improved blade geometry they provide. In my experience, fullers seriously detract from the blade's functional qualities. Let me explain.

One time many years ago, I was splitting an exceptional buck mule deer to ease the job of packing him out of rough country. I was alone, and a long way from my pickup. The knife I was carrying had a prominent fuller on both sides of the blade. It was a World War II surplus knife with no identifying marks.

I drove the blade between the animal's ribs and sternum and it hung up on the fullers. It was the only knife that I had and it was stuck. It took me a long time and a lot of work to get the blade loose. That was the last time I ever depended on a knife with a fullered blade.

Back to the parachutist knife. In my opinion, it is one of the most efficiently designed military knives. The blade spines are nicely rounded to make them user friendly. The drop point was thoughtfully designed and the cutting edge flows cleanly from the ricasso. There is nothing on the blade to hang up. I don't know who designed the knife, but it's nice to know that one man made something right and actually got the government to use it!

Parachutist knives are rare. Not many were made and they are expensive on the collector market—Larry Thomas said he recently sold one in mint condition for $1,800! The one I saw at the Blade Show was in outstanding condition. It's a shining example of what I consider a good knife that is definitely better than most.

Curves

French curve, a flat drafting instrument consisting of several scroll-like curves enabling a draftsman to draw curves of varying radii—Webster's Encyclopedia Unabridged Dictionary.

The first time I remember seeing a French curve, I was in fifth grade. Harry Truman was president and had just fired Gen. Douglas MacArthur. One of my friends had brought a majestic, yet aged, French curve to school and was tracing lines onto a piece of paper using the graceful curve as a guide. I was impressed. Never had I seen such simple beauty. I asked if I could use the French curve and my friend agreed. The next thing I knew, several hours had passed and the teacher was standing in front of my desk asking me a question. I hadn't heard a word he said. I was totally obsessed with the wondrous guide into the world of art that I held in my hands. The lines that came from her were beyond description, flowing gracefully from one smooth curve to the next. I felt that I had discovered a new land filled with unexplored territory that was waiting for me to discover its wonders.

My teacher confiscated the French curve and I felt that I had lost my most precious possession. I worried about its fate for the rest of the school day. After school, my friend and I begged for the return of the French curve. Upon its return, I promptly traded most of my worldly possessions - a stack of comic books and one well-used Barlow pocketknife for that old, faded piece of plastic that held the key to so much beauty. I spent countless hours tracing continuous curves on every piece of paper I could find. I knew by heart all of the French curve's graceful lines, as she became my avenue to beauty, my own private world of grace and nature.

I thought I was impressed by the beauty of her lines at that time, the significance of that old French curve's dynamics did not develop fully in my mind until I started seriously making knives years later. Like most knifemakers, I started with a lot of desire and very little knowledge about the direction my knifemaking would take.

Through other objects of art, knifemakers and craftsmen from times past have sent messages that touched me, telling of the splendor they saw and that they carefully blended into their creations. I knew there were aspects of their works that I had seen and felt were exceptionally attractive, but I did not completely understand why.

Slowly but surely, the secrets of the ancient craftsmen began to reveal themselves to me. One theme held my attention. I was unable to state exactly what it was that fascinated me, even though I was vaguely aware of any underlying theme in all the works that I admired.

The Common Denominator

Finally one day I began to realize that the lines of all great knife designs have one thing in common: curves. The

When it comes to knife curves, nobody has ever done it quite like the father of handmades, William Scagel (Photo courtesy of the Dr. James Lucie collection)

gentle, graceful lines that flowed from that first French curve were physically present in all of the art objects that I admired from the hands of countless craftsmen through the ages. My

Dr. James Lucoe was inspired by William Scagel and he has adopted some of Scagel's ideas into his own work. (Photo courtesy of the Dr, James Lucie collection)

fascination with the phenomenon of curves in knives developed as I experimented with the functional aspects of blade design. I soon learned that there is usually no requirement for a perfectly straight edge in a blade. Curves cut better and provide more cutting surface than do straight edges. Also, most straight edges are short lived and end up curved after they are used and resharpened several times.

For many years, I have studied what I consider to be the greatest examples of knifemaking of the past. I started out with a straight-edge ruler and tried to find straight lines in their designs. The results of these investigations revealed that while the curves might be ever so slight, there were virtually no straight lines in the designs that impressed me the most. I came to realize that all of the great knife designs that I had admired were present all the time in the lines of that first French curve.

The Beauty Of Curves

The beauty of curves stems from the fact that they are natural. I know of no straight lines coming from the hand of Mother Nature. Straight lines are a product of man. Straight lines appear cold and without function or beauty. There is no excuse for a straight line anywhere on a knife except on the cutting edge, and then only when there is a valid reason for it to be straight.

Examine all of the beauties of nature, from a spectacular sunrise to the symmetry of an eagle's wing. All of nature is curved. The beautiful women of all time and the dog that caresses your hand with equal devotion as you stroke her head consist of subtle, gentle, smooth-flowing, natural curves. Curves are kind, curves are natural and curves are beautiful. Curves speak of life to those who will hear.

How To Tell Good Knife Information From The Bad

There have been some harsh criticisms of forged blades and 52100 steel from various sources recently. When I read the critiques I did not take them seriously and did not feel that they were worth spending time to refute.

However, after talking with other knife enthusiasts and makers, I found that some newcomers took the criticisms seriously. Their questions and comments have prompted me to write the following.

In one of the critiques, 52100 was said to be unreliable and that it could break unexpectedly. 52100 is the steel of which most of the bearings used in all walks of life today are made. Civilization rides on 52100 steel. If it were less than reliable, another steel would be used instead. I have used 52100 exclusively in my knives for the past five years. I have forged many bearings into blades. I have given my blades every opportunity to fail, subjecting them to rigorous, destructive tests. I have found 52100 to be the cleanest, most uniform steel that I have ever used. Properly forged and heat treated, 52100 produces a high-performance blade that knows no peers. I have reached this conclusion based upon extensive personal research, testing knives for the things that they need to do in the real world of knife function.

All of these criticisms brings us to another point: How can the knife enthusiast avoid being taken in by those who promote knives that are in fact inferior? Remember that not everyone who writes about knives knows what he is talking about. Knifemakers and knife writers search for accurate information about steel. The most readily available information comes from the steel industry.

The steel industry has developed a language that uses a lot of big words that sound pretty darn official to the newcomer, Some of these terms become part of the language of knives. Since most of the technical terms have little or no meaning to most of the knife world, they can be used to lay down a significant smoke screen that will not only impress the average knife enthusiast, but may also be used to obscure significant issues that pertain to knife performance. For example: Should someone ask me a question about steel that I can't answer, all I have to do is digress into some esoteric discussion using exotic terms and the man seeking information will typically nod his head and change the subject. His question remains unanswered and my knowledge untested.

There is no need for highly technical terms when talking about knife function on a practical level. Only four relatively simple terms mean much when it comes to knife function:

1) <u>Strength</u>: the ability of a knife steel to resist bending
2) <u>Toughness</u>: a knife is tough when it can be bent and still maintain its ability to be used as a knife
3) <u>Abrasion Resistance</u>: a knife's ability to hold an edge
4) <u>Machinability</u>: how easily a knife can be sharpened

While entire books can be devoted to discussing any of these four terms, what they mean to the qualities of a truly high-performance knife is much simpler. Most of the time all that is needed in a knife is a blade that is strong, tough, holds

When evaluating a knife, find out how the maker tests his blades. When evaluating a knife story, note how the writer develops his information and reaches his conclusions. Here Rick Dunkerley performs the ABS free-hanging rope-cutting test with his master smith's test knife.

A knife is tough when it can be bent and still maintain its ability to be used as a knife.

an edge and is easy to sharpen. These qualities are easy to evaluate; all you have to do is use the knife.

I strongly feel that the most significant contribution to a knifemaker's ability is the degree that his testing program realistically relates to the required performance of his knives. Any maker who develops and uses a realistic testing program for his knives will in time make knives you can depend on. A knifemaker cannot rely solely on others to field test his knives. While field testing is important, just a small number of any maker's knives can be tested in the field. Effective quality control demands that every knife blade must pass some realistic tests; then a representative sample can be subjected to more rigorous tests, including those that destroy the knife.

The same principle applies to the quality of a knife writer's printed word. It is easy to regurgitate some technical terms from a metallurgy handbook in order to sound knowledgeable. The fact is that material from the steel industry was not intended to be indiscriminately applied to the knife world without the benefit of some realistic experimentation. Just because a certain steel or thermal treatment results in a quality cam shaft does not mean that the same process and material will make an acceptable knife.

When purchasing a using knife, ask the maker how he tests his knives and you will gain insight into the quality of his work. When reading about knives, examine the knives the author likes, ask yourself how he develops the information in his story, and evaluate his conclusions carefully.

A Special Knife For A Special Hand

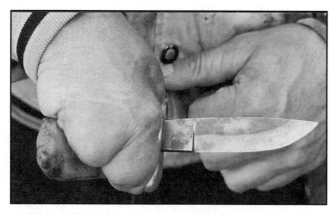

The brass guard provides a secure hold for applying force to the blade, and keeps Randy's hand from sliding onto the edge.

Randy Gerhardt has been our No. 1 hand at the Willow Bow Ranch for the past three years. He can do it all; his heart is big as all outdoors. He can spot a sick calf in a snowstorm and isn't above spending the night doctoring it when most hands would give up. It doesn't matter how cold it is or how long the day lasts-if there is work to be done, he will do it. Give him enough diesel fuel and a little bailing wire and he will keep a bailer running till the last windrow of hay is bailed. If he can't fix it in the field, it is a major breakdown. Randy was born to ranch work. He knows horses, cows, sheep and dogs like few men do. I've never known him to abuse an animal or lame up a horse. He takes care of the ranch, animals and equipment like they were his own. In short, he is a good hand.

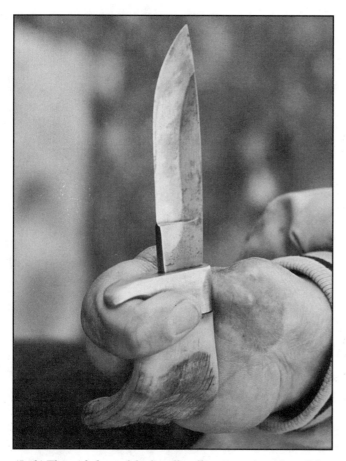

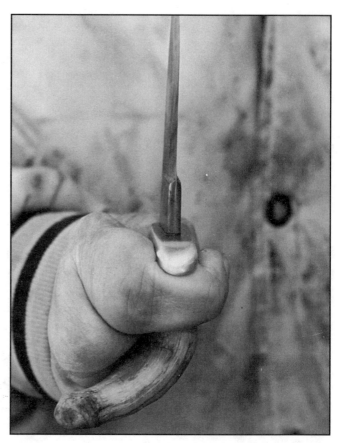

(Above) The tight curve of the horn handle wraps snugly around Randy's right hand. At age 7, Randy lost most of his hand in a hay bailer accident.

(Left) The wide butt of the handle offers a spacious "seat" for Randy's palm. The first job on which Randy used the knife was to skin out a calf that had died of pneumonia on the Willow Bow Ranch, and he made short work of it.

Randy was born right-handed but he didn't have much chance to be right-handed. He was 7 years old when he lost most of his right hand in a hay bailer accident. Since that time he has become proficient using his left hand and what is left of his right hand. I have never seen him unable to do what needs to be done.

Not long ago Randy found a sheep horn that had been knocked off one of our cross-bred buck sheep. The horn had a real tight curve in it. I noticed that Randy was holding it in his right hand and giving it some thought. I said, "That kind of looks like a knife handle." He smiled and said "Yeh!" Come Christmas time I asked Randy to pick through some knife blades that I had ready for handles. He picked one that he liked and we spent the next few weeks working out the design.

As he has only an index finger on his right hand with which to hold things, only he could figure out how to make the knife work. He held the piece of horn, thought about it, asked some questions and kept after it until the twinkle in his eye told me he had figured it out. The tight curve of the horn on the finished knife wraps snugly around his hand. The brass guard provides a secure hold for applying force to the blade and a wide margin of safety to keep his hand from sliding onto the edge and being cut.

It was a privilege to watch Randy hold the knife in his hand, a hand that couldn't hold and use a "normal" knife, and make his first cuts on a piece of aspen. The smile on his face was one of those special moments that a man will remember a long time.

It wasn't long and we had to skin a steer that had died. Randy used his knife and made short work skinning it out. The calf had died of pneumonia. We had spent a lot of time trying to pull it through, but it wasn't in the cards. Usually this kind of work isn't too palatable, but this day it was tempered with a new kind of success.

Knifesharpenophobia

Customers often ask, "How long can I cut with this knife until it needs sharpening?" For awhile I was plum ashamed to admit that my knives would ever need sharpening. I spent some time pondering the issue. Why the negative attitude toward sharpening knives? The knife is a tool. All tools need maintenance. That is the way with tools - it's the natural order of things. If you use something, maintain it. The more you use it, the more you maintain it. Caring for a knife is part of using it.

Granted, edge holding is a fine attribute for a knife. The problem is, knives that seldom need sharpening generally are usually too hard to sharpen when the time comes to sharpen them. They tend to be too brittle and aren't dependable. Having a broken blade is just as bad as being without a knife, and you're in worse shape than if you had a dull one. Why are knives with these faults so sought after?

I have concluded that the issue stems from a malady I call "Knifesharpenophobia." What is knifesharpenophobia? Webster defines phobia as "an irrational, excessive and persistent fear of some thing or situation." Knifesharpenophobia is a word previously found only in the Willow Bow Ranch dictionary of knife terms, written by yours truly. Since it is my word, I define it as an irrational, excessive and unnecessary fear of sharpening knives. This is a malady that strikes fear in the hearts of all too many knife lovers and users.

The fear develops at an early age. A youngster hears an adult say things like, "I can't sharpen a knife," or, "take these knives over to grandfather and ask him to sharpen them. He's the only one who can get a decent edge on a knife." The youngster comes to believe that sharpening a knife is one of those esoteric arts that is mastered only by the chosen few. The knife user who suffers from knifesharpenophobia not only misses the joy of using a truly sharp knife, he or she misses one of the enjoyable aspects of using a knife; namely, sharpening one.

I can still remember watching Dad standing at his workbench sharpening a knife. I asked him to sharpen mine and he did - not so sharp that it would cut much, especially me, but he worked it on a stone a little. I watched him sharpen, asked questions and he taught me the basics. I tried sharpening my own knives after that. I wasn't real successful at first, but with time and practice I sharpened a knife and it cut better than it did before I sharpened it. I was elated; this was one of my early tastes of success. Young maidens threw rose petals in my path and flags waved that day. Yeh!

It wasn't too long and I could put a shaving edge on any knife that was good enough. Other folks would use my knives and say, "Wow, would you sharpen mine?" That was a real sense of accomplishment.

Learning how to sharpen is like learning how to ride a bicycle. You try, you fall, then you try again. You keep on try-

14-a

ing and pretty soon you are riding like a pro. Maybe you aren't the best, but you get where you want to go. The same goes for sharpening knives. Maybe they won't be the sharpest in the world at first, but they will get the job done and every attempt is a learning experience. Anything is better than not trying!

There are training wheels for bicycles and there are training wheels for sharpening knives in the form of jigs and other devices. These help you build an excellent edge on your knife. The problem with these outfits it that, just as training wheels limit your ability to maneuver a bicycle, jigs and fixtures tend to limit your creativity when you wish to build the best cutting edge that your knife can support. Also, there may come a time when you need to sharpen a knife in the field and the training wheels are at home.

The only way to learn to sharpen is to practice. Pick up some old knives at the flea market, a garage sale or your kitchen. Make sure you aren't working on a valuable collector piece and then explore another area of satisfaction in the world of knives.

Examine the dull edge with a magnifying glass and compare it to a sharp edge. At first use any sharpening stone. Work the blade on the stone, look it over with the magnifying glass, try cutting with it and then give it another try. Review Wayne Goddard's "Q & A" column in the August 1991 "Blade Magazine," then try sharpening the edge again. If you need help, ask someone who knows how to give you a few pointers, then try again and again.

Next, buy some stones and try them or use your imagination. Knives can be sharpened on a lot of things: sandpaper placed on a piece of glass, or something with a smooth, hard surface such as smooth, flat rocks or smooth concrete. Experiment and have fun. The greatest single motivating factor to my sharpening ability came when I switched from a safety razor to a genuine straight-edge razor. That is when you definitely know you are successful at sharpening a piece of steel. If it isn't sharp, take time to make it sharp. Pretty soon, every morning you get to enjoy your skill and smile when you think about the money you are saving.

The point is this: Sharpening a knife can be just as much fun as using one. Sharpening is your opportunity to develop a skill and take over where the knifemaker leaves off. Sharpening is your signature on your knives. Owning a knife that can't be sharpened is like dating a picture rather than the real live lady. Sharpening knives is a skill that can be learned and, once you become proficient, is the source of a real sense of accomplishment.

Knife—Or Death!!

It was one of those late winter days in Wyoming when you knew that green grass was right around the corner and it was too hard to concentrate on work. The night-time temperature had dropped to somewhere around 20 degrees F. By 10 AM, warm winds had the cows stretched out on what bare ground they could find to enjoy the sun. I decided it was time that my dog, Blue, and I made our yearly trip across the frozen Wind River to an abandoned homestead, about a quarter mile from our ranch house. Three months of below-zero temperatures had provided a good foot of ice covering the river. Crossing was easy; the temperature was still below freezing and the ice afforded plenty of traction.

We spent most of the day looking at tracks and bedding grounds of the wildlife that usually winters there. It wasn't long and the snow started melting. Blue was having fun nosing some rabbits out of the brush. Usually when I try to take a nap in the afternoon, the phone rings. The day was perfect and, being far from the phone, I figured I could catch a few winks. I knew that Blue would wake me in plenty of time to get back and feed the animals-she being one of those animals. Faithful to the duties of being No. 1 girl and ranch dog, she woke me at about 2 PM.

We walked back to the river and started across. Usually I like to carry a fair-sized stick when walking on ice to help keep my balance. This day there wasn't one nearby. Rather than take the time to find a suitable walking stick, I decided I could get along without one. As we started across, I noticed the water was just starting to melt on top of the ice. About the third step I took my feet slid out from under me and I wound up flat on the ice, slowly inching downstream. Blue came over to me, having little trouble digging her claws into the ice. She licked my face and stood there waiting for me to get up. Trouble was, there was a co-efficient of friction that was about as close to zero as anything I had ever tried to walk on. I could stand but I just kept slowly sliding downstream. The ice in the middle of the river was lower than the ice on the banks and that is where I ended up, slowly headed downstream.

I tried laying down and rolling toward the bank on the 'home' side of the river bank but that didn't work. I tried crawling on my hands and knees; that didn't work either. Had I picked up that stick like I usually did, it probably would have helped me get back to the bank, but I didn't have one. No matter what I tried, the result was the same—I was headed downstream. At this point I thought the situation kind of comical, one of those predicaments Red Skelton or Charlie Chaplin would have jumped all over. The cows were home waiting to be fed and the main cook was playing on the ice!

Then I became aware of open water about 100 yards downstream from me, a patch of water about the size of my living room emerging from under the ice then disappearing

under the ice again for as far as I could see. The urgency of the situation became immediately clear. I called Blue over and took hold of her tail to see if she could tow me. She tried but her claws didn't provide enough traction to move the two of us. I scanned the banks hoping to locate a tree branch that I could have Blue retrieve, but no luck.

It was time to try anything. I pulled my knife from its sheath and stuck it in the ice. Right hand on the handle, I grabbed the blade with my left hand. My progress downstream stopped! I pulled on the knife and was on my way toward the bank. It took a while but we made it. I was surprised how little effort it took to pull myself across the ice. It didn't take much to get me out of the fix that my own stupidity got me into, but I was pretty proud of the fact that what I had was good enough.

Did the knife save my life? I honestly don't know; I might have quit moving downstream before sliding into the open water and being pulled under the ice, or I could have waited until the night-time temperature again froze the surface of the ice. A lot of "ifs!" I know one thing: I don't plan on trying the same stunt again.

Avoid Knife Accidents: Here's How

A knifemaker and a friend from Casper, Wyoming, recently stopped by my shop to partake in the kind of knife talk that occurs when two knifemakers get together. The conversation got around to guards. I am a firm believer in full guards when it comes to knives to be carried in the field. All sheath knives that I carry have full guards; most of the knives that I make have full guards.

My friend stated that he was getting away from making knives with full guards because some of his customers had complained that the full guard got in the way, preventing full use of the knife. For a brief second I felt a little anxiety concerning my staunch support of the full guard on the using knife in the field. I feel that the full guard provides a measure of safety that is extremely advantageous. My own use had not revealed any negative aspects that can not be overcome with a little practice. With more than mild curiosity I asked my knifemaking friend what his customers were doing when the guard hindered their use of the knife.

He then held one of my knives with a full guard in his hand, holding it in the same manner as one would hold a ski pole, blade down, with the edge pointing back toward his elbow. It was the grip one of his customers used when finding the full guard objectionable. He also stated that his customer was opening the chest of a deer when he used this grip. I took the knife in my hand and the guard did dig into the palm of my hand! I asked myself, why hadn't I noticed this before? I butcher many animals every year and had never noticed any discomfort. It then came to me that I don't cut that way with a knife!

When opening an animal's chest cavity, the cartilage between the sternum and the ribs can be tough to locate. Older animals have less cartilage and more bone and are tougher to open. The tougher the cut, the more force you have to apply. When you apply a greater amount of muscle power into the cutting action of a knife, it is very easy to cut through suddenly or pull out of the material you are cutting. Should you be cutting toward your body, you will have the knife coming at you with a lot of momentum. You guessed it—cutting toward yourself is hazardous to your health.

When I was 6 years old, my grandmother taught me never to cut toward myself. She was teaching me how to peel potatoes; I can still hear her words: "Don't ever cut toward yourself with a knife, or you will cut yourself." I tried it her way and it seemed more difficult. She looked the other way and I turned the knife around and sure enough, I cut myself.

When you use a knife safely, a full guard doesn't get in your way. But when you use a knife the wrong way, the guard is a subtle reminder that you are cutting incorrectly. A local story underlines my point. Andy Davidson, the ranch's right-hand man, and I were working in the shop when the following news came over the radio. An elk hunter who had been re-

ported missing earlier had been found dead. He was lying beside a partially dressed-out elk carcass. He had been dressing the animal, evidently pulling the knife toward himself, and had driven the knife into his thigh, severing the femoral artery. He bled to death. He had tried to place a tourniquet on his leg but was unable to stop the flow of blood. He was 32 years old.

You have just read what prompted me to write this article. Knife safety is something we all know about. The trouble is, when you are working in what is to you a novel situation, you tend to forget the obvious. Should we watch someone else solve a problem by using poor methods but getting results, we sometimes adopt those methods ourselves no matter how unsafe they may be.

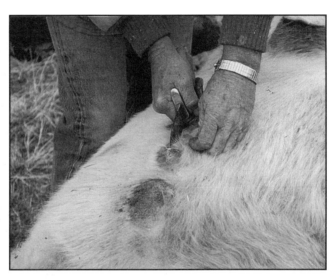

(Above) Note that the knife is being pushed away from the user's body during cutting, not toward the user.

Safety: The Rules

Based on my experience with, knives, hunting and human nature, these are my thoughts on knife safety in the field:

1. Always cut in a safe direction. You don't point a firearm at yourself or anyone else-the same principle applies to a knife. The act of dressing out an animal in the field can be accomplished safely and with efficient speed. Use your head and take your time.

2. When using a new knife, be extra careful until you get used to it. Many accidents happen when someone is cutting with a new or recently sharpened knife. Whenever I sharpen a knife for someone, I suggest that he take it easy with the knife until he gets used to it.

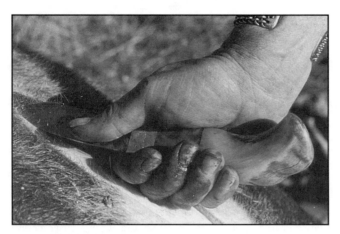

(Above) The full guard keeps the hand from slipping forward onto the edge during cutting.

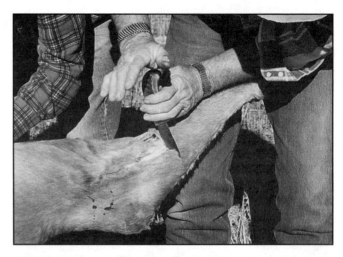

(Above) When the going gets tough, start the blade under the hide and drive the knife through the hide by hitting the butt with the palm of your other hand.

I learned No. 2 the hard way. I work on the kill floor at a local packing plant on occasion. One day I took some newly designed blades with me in order to test them out. One of the guys working there was an old pro, and he liked one of the knives and wanted to try it out. I was bending over the cow cutting on the inside of a front leg, and he was just starting to open her up. The knife that he had been using cut with quite a bit of drag compared to the knife I gave him to use. I finished my cut and stood up; just as I stood up, he cut through the cow's hide and the knife made a powerful arc, passing the spot where my head had been. Our eyes met, both of us realizing the significance of what had just happened. He said "That knife is too sharp!" He then took part of the edge off on his steel and went back to work. That was very close to being a serious accident. I had inadvertently set him up. I should have stood back and allowed him the opportunity to get used to the knife first. With the preceding in mind:

3. Watch out for the other guy. Two people dressing or skinning the same animal tend to cross paths regularly.

4. When helping someone else dress an animal, let the other person know before making any changes in the animal's position. (A good friend of mine permanently lost the use of a finger when his hunting partner got a little heavy handed trying to break open a joint on the leg opposite the one my friend was skinning.)

5. Don't be in a rush; meat won't spoil during the extra time it takes to do the job safely.

6. Be prepared for accidents. Everyone should take a first-aid course. Any member of your family or hunting party could be called upon to provide emergency care in a life-threatening situation. First you need to know what to do, then you must be mentally ready to act. A call to the Red Cross, county health department, local hospital or your family physician should be adequate to provide you with the time and location of the next first-aid course in your area. The above provide the knowledge, but it is up to you to be prepared for action. I try to keep myself ready to act in an emergency situation by fantasizing what could occur.

First-aid kits are available at most drug stores. You should have one in your home, car and camp. I carry a packet of surgical suture material with a cutting needle in my billfold. It comes in handy when I need to sew up animals or myself. I also carry some antibiotic powder and a tube of Superglue in my saddlebags. Band-Aids take up little room in your billfold. Saddlebags or backpacks should also contain

(Above) This is the most dangerous grip you can use in the field. All of the action is toward your body; one slip and you could be in trouble.

(Above) A sharp knife is essential and I sharpen mine on a genuine, smooth Wyoming rock.

Accident Prevention

Accident prevention is the name of the game. Remember the basics. Knives can cut, that is their job.

1. When using a knife in the field, don't pull toward you, push. Watch out for the other guy.

2. Get used to your knife before you use it; take your time and get to know it well.

3. Know the basic elements of first aid. Avoid accidents, but be ready for them.

4. Keep yourself emotionally ready to act. The role playing I mentioned is the best method.

5. Thorough planning-cover all the bases.

bandages for use on humans or animals. Talk to your family physician and veterinarian to help you lay in a supply of the "right stuff." Also, ask him to share his views on emergency first-aid. Always carry the bare necessities on your person.

Cutting yourself is no pleasant situation. When I started making knives I cut myself with enough frequency that I became rather proficient at stitching my own "hide," purely due to economic factors. When you cut yourself in the field, the most important factor is not to panic. You have already screwed up, but it's happened; now it's up to you to make the best of it.

Shock is a number one killer in these situations; you need to act, not bury your head in the sand. To help avoid shock, apply some direct pressure to the wound in order to reduce blood loss, then sit down and get your head between your knees and think what you are going to do next. I have seen people pass out over wounds that required little more than a Band-Aid. You can't afford that when you are the one to handle the situation. Should you pass out before you shut down heavy blood loss, you won't wake up. The roll playing previously mentioned can be a great asset. The blood on the ground is "spilled milk". You need to be concerned with keeping the blood that is still in your body. As soon as you can, apply the treatment you learned in first-aid.

Through The Eyes Of A Master Smith

Those who have lived lives filled with curiosity about the dynamics of man's tools, examining all the details that have come to their eyes and dedicating themselves to making a better knife, bring a special gift to all who love and live blades. Makers who have dedicated themselves to the functional knife are a breed apart.

As an American Bladesmith Society master smith, testing the knife performance qualities of the applicants seeking journeyman and master smith ratings is part of my responsibilities. I consider myself very fortunate, for I have never had to fail an applicant on the basis of a test blade's performance. ABS members who have come to my shop to test their knives have all been highly dedicated makers who, by virtue of their dedication to the functional blade, have done the homework required in developing high-performance knives.

Under the steady gaze of the author (left), applicant Kirk Rexroat performs the two-by-four cutting test.

Most applicants have called several times before the day of the test. Together, we have discussed at length how to build and test knives that will display the attributes necessary to pass the test. Meanwhile, the applicants have perfected the qualities of their blades well before the day of the actual test.

Zero Hour

Recently, an applicant for the journeyman smith rating came to my shop to put his blade through the performance portion of the test. Prior to this, he had called and visited me several times to talk knives.

The day of the test, I met him as he walked up to my shop. I asked him if he was ready. The look of confidence in his eye told me that he was not only ready, he was anxious to show what his knife could do.

I asked him about the steel and how the blade had been heat treated. Again, with all the confidence the eye can reveal, he told me that the steel was 5160 subjected to a large degree of forging. He said the blade had undergone all the right thermal treatments, including a multiple quench. He stated that he had made several blades at the same time. He had tested the other knives on his own before coming to my shop, and they had passed the test. He had made the untested blade along with those that had passed the test, and he handed me the knives for my evaluation. I looked at a blade that he said already had passed the ABS performance test. It had retained a 15° bend following the 90° flex test, and the cutting edge had experienced no perceptible wear whatsoever.

He handed me his test knife. I took my time looking it over. Careful examination divulged that everything was right about it. He had etched the blade, revealing what appeared to be a perfect heat-treatment system. The etch on the lower third of the edge showed an ultrafine grain structure. There was a transition area in the middle of the blade exhibiting increasingly coarser grain structure. The etch on the back of the blade had a coarse grain, indicating that it was very near to being dead soft. Close scrutiny of the cutting edge revealed that its geometry was well planned and executed.

As mentioned, the applicant had called me several times prior to the test. Whenever an applicant calls concerning the testing procedure, I take enough time to thoroughly describe what the ABS expects. I also suggest additional qualities that, while not necessary to pass the test, I would like to see in the performance of a knife that will make it superior to most of the blades made today. After examining his knife, I was confident that it would pass the test with ease.

Free-Hanging Rope Cut

We proceeded with the first portion of the performance test. He had brought about 20 feet of 1-inch hemp rope to use in the free-hanging, rope-cutting test. The test blade cannot be over 11 inches long. This blade was about 10 inches long.

I hung the rope over a rafter in my shop and the applicant made his first cut. The ABS journeyman smith test requires that a length of about 6 inches be cut from the free-hanging rope. His first cut took about 3 inches off the end of the rope. The more rope you cut from the larger piece, the less the requirement for precision rope-cutting edge geometry. I have seen very few blades capable of this level of performance. He said that he had cut quite a bit of rope before coming to my shop. This was an understatement to say the least! He was more than well prepared for this portion of the test.

Two-by-Four Test

Following the rope cut, he cut through the seasoned pine two-by-four twice with ease. The severed portions of the two-by-four looked polished, indicating they had been cut with a truly premium edge. Not only would the blade still easily shave hair, there was virtually no wear to the cutting edge (and this was by inspection under high magnification). He and another applicant for journeyman smith-Audra Draper, who has been an apprentice in my shop for the past three years-then engaged in some extended knife talk and conducted a few extra tests on the blade. Their dedication to knife function was music to my ears.

The 90° Flex

We proceeded to the 90° flex test. The applicant placed the test blade in my vise and flexed it to 90° . The result was the expected ideal level of performance. The blade was strong, resisting the flex, yet it still flexed throughout its full length to the required 90° As he relaxed the tension on the blade, it returned to within 25° of straight.

Outside the author's shop, applicant Rick Dunkerley bends his blade in a vise to 90 degrees in the flex test.

The creation of high-performance knives comes from the heart of the maker. Nothing comes easy, and the dedication of those who decide to attempt becoming an ABS journeyman and then master smith are a credit to the society and to those who appreciate the value of blades that can go the extra mile.

Only twice in the member bladesmith's career will the ABS test his/her work: once for journeyman and once for master smith status. These are only stepping stones. From that point on the test becomes much more severe-the test of each smith's heart to continue the search for the "Excalibur" of the 20th century and beyond. It all starts with the heart and birth of a maker who seeks something better. I thank those who have come to my shop over the phone lines, in letters and in person to bring joy to my heart in the quest for better knives.

The following are ABS journeyman smith basic requirements, for more information contact the ABS.

An applicant who wishes to be certified as an ABS journeyman smith must complete a three-phase qualification procedure based on 1) ABS membership and forging experience; 2) forging a test blade that will pass the cutting, chopping and bending tests; and 3) making finished knives that pass examination by the ABS board of judges.

I. The applicant must be a regular member (apprentice smith) of the ABS for at least two years prior to earning his journeyman rating.

II. The applicant must forge a test blade about 10 inches long and present the blade in person at the shop of an ABS master smith for testing.

A. All cutting, chopping and bending tests must be performed by the applicant.

B. The blade must first cut a free-hanging, 1-inch hemp rope about 6 inches from the loose end, completely severing the rope with one stroke of the test knife.

C. The applicant, using the same test blade, must then cut a two-by-four in two at least twice. Upon completion, the test blade must be capable of shaving hair from the applicant's arm.

D. After the cutting and chopping tests have been successfully completed, the applicant must clamp the test blade in a vise and bend the blade to at least 90°. The blade must not break. The edge is allowed to crack, but the back must remain intact.

E. The master smith may require the applicant to forge a blade in a given style to demonstrate that the applicant knows the proper techniques of forging a blade to shape.

NOTE: If the applicant does not successfully pass the above tests, a six-month waiting period is required before retesting.

CHAPTER 2

Knife Talk Philosophy

There is a lot to knives, so there also has to be more to people. These thoughts refer to the "knifropomorphic"* aspects of our favorite tool, friend and lover, lady knife. There have been and are a lot of people in the world of knives. I have tried to recognize a few of them, most importantly, I sought to shine a little light on the what I feel it was that made them special citizens in the world of knives.

* Knifropormorphic, the ascribing of human characteristics particularly social, romantic and mental, to knives. Taken from the "Ed Fowler world of knives dictionary."

That First Knife

When I first entered the world of knives, I couldn't read or write. I was without funds, education or any means of support. I had no money of my own and depended totally on the generosity of people who knew and helped me. In short, I was a little kid. When I was given my first rubber knife at the age of three or four, I was rich beyond my wildest dreams. I can still remember that knife, how proud I was with it stuffed into my belt as I rode my tricycle around the block with my tin star stuck on my shirt. It did not matter that it wouldn't cut, nor did it disappoint me when I threw it at a tree and it bounced off. That old rubber knife was my prize possession, my key to survival. Daniel Boone, Davy Crockett and I all walked together!

I still enjoyed the memories it brought back thirty years later when I found the rubber knife, still scarred with puppy teeth marks, well used in my children's toy box. It raised me, two of my kids and many other children who played with it.

Everyone who enters the world of knives with his/her first knife feels something special, though the feeling involves more than just a knife. The piece may be made of plastic, wood or rubber, or maybe even steel. The event and the blade become noteworthy because they are part of something more, maybe a need or a dream associated with someone held dear. The giver of the knife may be a parent, grandparent or a friend. Whenever one gives another a blade, a bond is formed between the giver and the recipient that can never be broken.

I still remember the day my grandfather gave me that first real knife. It wasn't expensive. I was a kid and didn't need anything costly; just a blade was all it had to be. It was a gift I'll never forget.

Entry Level Knives

Any first knife of consequence to the owner or maker is what I call the entry-level knife for that person. An entry-level blade opens the door to the world of knives for the newcomer. While my first blade was a gift from my grandfather, many others of little quality followed. They were bought at the dime store, bargain bin at the hardware store, army-surplus store or secondhand. They didn't cost much and didn't last very long. The handles broke, the blades loosened up or snapped, sometimes the handles came off, and most of them didn't hold an edge very long. Still, each new knife, regardless of quality, was a new adventure then as it is now.

Time has changed my interests. The blades I add to my collection come to my attenion for different reasons. Still, the fascination continues. Each new knife is a new adventure, a new friend and new memories.

Pocketknives with unsharpened edges, such as this Hopalong Cassidy Character Knife from Smoky Mountain Knife Works held by Dustin Unkle, are an example of entry-level pieces. (Fowler photo)

The author's rubber knife and tin star represent memories he will cherish forever. (Fowler photo)

Was it that first rubber blade that started my love affair with knives, or was it my interest in blades that brought us together? Who knows? What difference does it make which came first? All that matters is that a kid and a knife came together and it was all because someone thought to make an entry-level blade. It had all the desirable attributes: it looked like a knife, it was safe, cheap, available and, best of all, it was mine!

There are as many reasons for a knife as there are makers and people who buy blades. Many knives are not intended, nor are they supposed, to be highly superior. They are made by beginning craftsmen or are the product of mass production designed to fill the needs of the customer who neither wants, needs nor can afford the top of the line. They are not made to provide the man who requires and will use a working blade with a quality product. Rather, they are made for the customer who wants to fill a need without investing a lot of hard-earned cash.

The "Ultimate Survival Knife"

It wasn't too long ago that I saw the "ultimate survival knife" advertised on TV. It had all the hopes, smells and tastes of the annual circus parade that you could imagine. There was a compass, saw, can opener, bottle opener, hollow handle filled with "survival gear," and even a cutting edge. It sold for less than $20, including a genuine leather sheath, and was "guaranteed."

I even saw the blade used by a tough guy on a TV show. He and the knife lived up to all the implied glories. Not too long after that, a young man rode to my shop on his bicycle and wanted me to sharpen one of the "ultimate survival knives" that he had bought. The only part of the piece that really worked was the bottle opener. I put the best edge the knife could support on the blade and advised him that it wasn't going to last very long. He said, "I know that but I like the knife anyway!"

I don't think the $20 blade was misrepresented. It filled a need and kept some money flowing in the economy, and obviously provided the buyer with some pleasure. A lot of entry-level knives surrounded by glorious advertising are bought and sold in the marketplace. There's nothing wrong with a part of the cutlery industry supplying an entry-level product for tomorrow's blade enthusiast. Entry-level knives are special. They don't have to cut, be practical, last very long or be pretty. All they have to do is fit into someone's dream.

Caveman Cutler

When I judge a knife, function and safety are the two most important considerations. Then comes creativity resulting in knives that tell it like it is, but with style, made by knifemakers who have the imagination and courage to do it "their way." Attend any show and you will see thousands of knives. Many of those knives look like peas in a pod. Cover the names of the makers, mix the knives around, then try to identify who made what. Your level of success on many would not be much greater than that dictated by pure chance.

This is a typical stone-age knife, thought to have been chipped by stone-age man in the vicinity of Copper Mountain in Fremont County, Wyoming. It is a beautiful piece, sharp top and bottom, with a tang for handle attachment. When using this knife, a man would not have been able to apply any pressure on the top of the edge because it is as sharp as the bottom edge.

This is unfortunate. The knife is a tool. It is used for cutting, chopping, scraping and sticking. These are pretty simple duties, providing thousands of opportunities for the maker to creatively express himself. When a new maker asks me what it takes to be a great maker, he is in for a lengthy discussion concerning all aspects of knifemaking. I then suggest that he try to enhance his individuality by creating a knife that is readily recognizable as coming from his own hands.

In order to preserve my hide, I won't mention any makers by name. Just choose a few. Sit back and consider those makers who have distinguished themselves and their customers by crafting functional, creative knives that set themselves apart from the rest of the herd by their individuality. These are the craftsmen whose knives will live on to be cherished for generations to come.

Some time ago, my good friend Ray Parman, author of "Rare and Unusual Artifacts of the First Americans" (ISBN No. 0-9623868-0-4), provided me the privilege of examining a knife that was made by a person who may have been one of the truly great makers of prehistory. I have seen a great many stone-age knives. I own some real beauties. Most of them are memorable due to the material of which they are made and by the craftsmanship of the maker. However, most of them appear to have been designed by the same person. The style of chipping varies over thousands of years but they are all essentially double-edge knives. I tried a double-edge knife on big game, once. That was enough!

I have always wondered why greater individual differences in stone-age knives don't seem to exist. Surely some stone-age maker thought for himself! The knife that Parman displayed for my observation immediately stood out as a one-of-a-kind example of a true craftsman's individual creativity. Examining that knife is a moment that remains with a man in spirit forever.

The knife's banded chert is as beautiful as any. The chipping is high quality workmanship. The functional aspects of the design soar with the eagles and firmly rank this knife in a class by itself. The cutting edge is a precision instrument. (The damage near the tip was probably incurred after the knife was made.) The top of the blade is straight and clean, efficiently dropping to the tip. The back is gracefully and comfortably rounded on the right side, and the left side is an excellent scraper. The person using this knife could have placed his thumb on the spine of the blade in order to increase his leverage to the cutting edge, and thereby lessen fatigue without having to place his thumb on a sharp edge. This would also reduce the strain on the point of attachment between the blade and the handle, as well as reducing stress on the blade itself. One blade, two tools; a highly functional knife and scraper!

Another stone-age knife found on the Willow Bow Ranch, Fremont County, Wyoming. Approximately one-fourth of this knife is missing. Still, you can see the double-edge blade.

Viewing the blade from the right side, you can see that the tool is actually a scraper. It was used much like a draw knife. Two tools in one, an excellent knife and a scraper. The rounded top edge is user friendly for a man's thumb.

Why this idea didn't take the prehistoric world by fire and storm I can only hazard a few guesses. Tradition may have prevented others from accepting the design's virtues or, due to the fact that news didn't spread too far or rapidly in those days, the idea may have been laid to rest with the original maker, waiting thousands of years to be picked up on the Wyoming prairie.

Whoever he was, I tip my Stetson to the man who thousands of years ago did his own thing and created an original statement of art and function. I will never meet him in this life but hope to meet him one day in the next. One thing's sure: If we both end up in the same place, I will look him up.

How You Can Ensure The Future Of Knives!

Will Christopher Scott (here making a wood knife with the help of his "Melissa-powered" grinder) one day grow up to be a master knifemaker or will he become disillusioned? The answer may depend on you.

One thing we all have in common is that each of us made his/her first knife. Some started early, some started late in life, but they all remember that first knife. It may be that they remember early knives of clay or wood, but that first knife of steel is a memorable occasion. A great many knifemakers still own that first knife of steel, and there may even be a scar or two to support that memory.

A knifemaker's ego is born with that first knife, whether he/she is 4 years old or 70. I have seen adult men more excited over their first knife than a kid with his first puppy. That ego is tender; it is easily bruised and will also remember its first caress forever. Just like other aspects in everybody's lives, it takes seven "attaboys" just to negate one "yea, but..."

The first time I showed one of my knives to a big-name knifemaker he put me down hard. To this day I still remember the sting of his words and how I felt. Don't get me wrong; criticism is vital to a knifemaker's growth. It is just more palatable when it is served with sugar rather than grit.

The same day that I got my feelings hurt, I met Bill Moran for the first time. I had seen pictures of Bill in the magazines and was anxious to meet him in person. I walked up, looked at his knives and introduced myself. Bill's kind eye and friendly nature welcomed me to his world. We talked knives and I felt welcome. Bill eyed the knife on my belt and asked if I had made it. I replied "yes" and hurriedly added, "it isn't too good." Bill asked to see it and I gingerly handed it to him. He took his time, looked my knife over carefully and proceeded to say a lot of nice things about it. He discussed the advantages of the forged blade and invited me to attend one of his classes.

Here I was, a rank beginner, talking to one of the great knifemakers of our time and he not only had the time to talk to me, he demonstrated a genuine interest in me and my knives. There were a lot of things wrong with that knife; Bill Moran knew it and I knew it. Our discussion focused on positive aspects of knives, past, present and future. Bill had the time to share with me and showed a genuine interest in me and my knives. It was because of Bill's attitude toward me that I became a member of the American Bladesmith Society. I felt like I had a new set of friends and family. That feeling persists today.

"Bill Moran's kind eye and friendly nature welcomed me to his world. We talked knives and I felt welcome. Bill eyed the knife on my belt and asked if I had made it... He took his time, looked my knife over carefully and proceeded to say a lot of nice things about it."

This is how new knifemakers become old timers. It is because we have the interest and someone takes an interest in us. This concept isn't limited to knifemakers. Included are collectors, one-time buyers and folks who just plain are interested in knives. Whenever anyone calls or walks up to those of us who have a little knowledge about knives and asks a question or shows us one of those primitive first-time knives, we are ensuring the future of knives by sharing time with them, showing a genuine interest in them and their ideas, and welcoming them to the fold.

Knifemakers need not fear competition. If they do their homework and make an honest knife, there will be a market for knives.

I feel that my greatest competition is with myself. I am thrilled and honored when those I help and teach excel. If each of us in the world of knives brings 10 new folks into the fold, our future will be ensured and the world of knives will continue to prosper and grow. Each new convert brings with him or her a fresh new set of experiences and friends that will enrich a pretty nice place: the world of knives.

Just Your Imagination...

"Imagination is greater than knowledge"...These words were on a bumper sticker, the quote attributed to Albert Einstein. I saw it in the morning and thought about it all day.

Imagination is greater than knowledge—what does that have to do with knives? A lot when you think about it. Consider all of the knives you have seen down through the years. Doubtless some come readily to mind. You can see them in your mind's eye, almost touch them.

Some knives stand out due to the circumstances surrounding their use. Knives in this category may or may not be great in and of themselves. Any knife can earn a place in your heart when it is the tool used in a time of great need, such as the knife that Uncle Harvey used to kill a bear or grandmother's favorite potato peeling knife.

Other knives that fit this category are ones given to you by a special friend, such as the knife your grandfather gave you. My grandfather gave me my first pocketknife. Today I remember that knife as well as the day he gave it to me over 45 years ago. Other knives that stand out may have been used by the legendary Jim Bowie or Davy Crockett. These are knives that are special simply due to the history or legend that surrounds them.

Then there are the knives that stand out due to a combination of legend and the materials used in their construction. Again, the Bowie legend comes to mind. James Black supposedly forged a blade using a meteorite in the steel, giving Jim Bowie a blade from heaven-or hell and earth. This thought still holds some of us spellbound. The Bowie legend and the knives that were designed and sold claiming to be a part of that legend extend through to the Civil War and the streets of many cities, to the canyons and hilltops of the country. The knives made it into the imaginations of the young boys and men who read about them in newspapers and paperback books. The more they read and heard, the greater the need and significance of a Bowie in their lives became. *(Notice how imagination is playing a part in this discussion so far?)*

Another aspect of knives and imagination comes to mind when you consider knives that are constructed from expensive materials combined with highly superior workmanship. The most significant of these in recent times is the replica of the King Tut dagger made by Buster Warenski. For some there is a legend behind the dagger, but for me at least the workmanship and materials totally surpass the legend. The Tut dagger exhibits sheer beauty beyond description. Credit must be given to the man who afforded the opportunity and to the man who had the dedication, ability and courage to put it all together.

Now consider knives made of standard materials but due to their nature come to mind as art/combat knives. Gil Hibben is one of the kings of this realm. Others also come to mind,

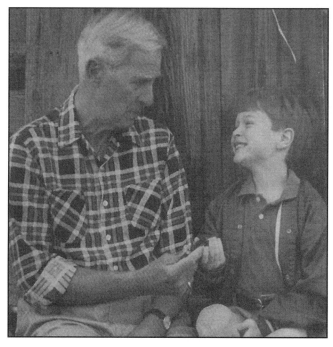

"... knives that fit this category are ones given to you by a special friend, such as your grandfather." The author remembers the knife his granddad gave to him 45 years ago. Here O.L. Shackleford gives a pocketknife to his grandson, Mike Howell.

such as Jimmy Lile and his Rambo series. These are knives that, given a little encouragement by their promoters and your imagination, do more to inspire you than they could otherwise. Imagination lets you slay dragons and conquer infinitely superior foes. Just having such a knife in the house makes you feel a little better, stand a little taller, maybe even wish someone would come along and kick sand in your face. Walter Mitty lives in us all.

Bob Loveless came along with some imagination and made knives that set a lot of hearts to thumping. His designs are seen in many other makers' styles. Simplicity, grace, clean, attractive lines, something a little different that works.

Look at what William Wales Scagel did in the first half of the 20th century with a hammer, anvil and a little imagination. His knives are, and always will be, highly sought after. Their value comes from within, gained from the nourishment that his creativity instilled. They stand on their own merits.

There are knives that are what they are and a whole lot more. Bill Moran made a good knife but he wanted to make more than a knife; he wanted to preserve a way of making a better knife, not only his knives, but all forged knives. He did his homework, made Damascus steel and shared his knowledge with others, creating a new organization (the American Bladesmith Society) dedicated to the preservation and promotion of the forged blade. By sharing his knowledge Bill gave his students the best of over 50 years of experience right out of the starting gate. He hand-picked the individuals to carry his ideas long beyond his time. Bill, his knives and his friends are the start of a new era in the world of knives.

Paul Burke Jr. never made a knife, but his guidance has given the ABS a clean start. Burke, the rest of the ABS board of directors, and Moran and his knives have come together to build something much greater than knives alone. Still, the knives symbolize the whole. Without Bill's knives setting the table, the ABS would not have been created.

Frank J. Richtig made knives from 1926-76. He invested his time and developed a heat treating method that produced blades that are still better than most. From what I hear the knowledge came only after a significant amount of effort on his part. He then promoted his knives with enthusiasm. He didn't have to tear anyone else down, he just showed what his knives would do. This is imagination at its best. An entire nation read about Richtig and his knives in the "Ripley's Believe It Or Not" feature of the comic pages in the Sunday newspaper.

Imagination is greater than knowledge, though without knowledge imagination either runs wild or doesn't exist. Knowledge supports imagination. Without knowledge these men's knives would have lacked foundation. Without imagination they would have never been noticed. Combine knowledge gained through the quest for information, driven by a hunger that is never satisfied and tempered with imagination, and you have a great knifemaker and a great knife.

Knives Tell Stories

The original owner smoothed out the edges of the guard on his Marble's Woodcraft to better fit his hand during knife use.

Whenever a man uses a knife, there's a history for others to enjoy when they read the story left in the knife. Some fine old knives have been subjected to blatant abuse by errant idiots who had no respect for one of man's most widely used tools. The knives bear the scars of abuse that could have no purpose other than to serve insanity bent on destruction. I enjoy cleaning these "fine old ladies" and giving them another chance to serve mankind.

The greatest treasures of all are the knives used by men who obviously got the most out of them. The blades have been used extensively, sharpened with a definite purpose in mind. Many times, modifications to the original design have made the knife friendlier to the hand that used it. Such knives are a wealth of information to those who study them with open hearts.

Through the years I have accumulated quite a few of the Woodcraft-style knives. Marble's usually get credit for the first one—I have seen similar knives made long before the Marble's model—then many other manufacturers made versions. I have Woodcraft-style knives made by Marble's, Case, Kinfolks, Ka-Bar and other makers great and small. While many Woodcraft types in mint condition are somewhat expensive, those that interest me usually are in a lot less than mint condition and are pretty affordable.

The other day I came across a fine old Marble's Woodcraft that had seen a lot of use. Laying in the display case at Jake's Trading Post, she looked more accommodating than my favorite old boots. I examined her closely and found that she had been cared for by a man who knew how to get the most from a knife.

The first and most obvious change he made to her blade was an altered edge profile, making her slightly more pointed with less belly. This made her better for sticking and safer to use when greater power was needed. She would still be an adequate skinning blade but not as likely to pull out of a tough cut. The second change was the carefully honed edge geometry. Rather than a consistently thin slicing edge, he had carefully increased the sharpening angle to provide a stronger edge than she had when she left the factory.

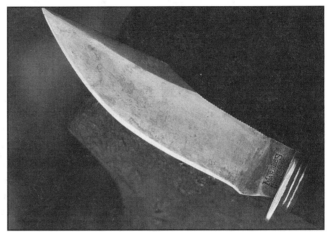

Note the superb edge geometry. The man who reground and sharpened the edge knew what he wanted and how to get it.

On the spine of the blade he had smoothed out the serrated thumb rest. Serrated spines and other filework on the blade's back are popular with the armchair knife fraternity because they provide a non-slip area on which the user's thumb may ride. While these notches may feel nice in the store or at the knife show, they tend to rasp through the skin of your thumb during serious knife use.

The owner smoothed out the thumb ridges on the Woodcrafts' blade spine to make the ridges easier on his thumb during use.

The owner had also carefully rounded the edges of the guard to make it more receptive to his hand. Sharp guards-like sharp serrations on the blade spine-can make for sore fingers in a short time when you use a knife for extended periods. In addition, he had removed the retaining nut and pommel from the handle and oiled the concealed tang to prevent rust.

The fine old Marble's knife was paired with a Knapp Saw. Our knife lover had taken the keeper strap off the original sheath and added it to the saw's sheath. With his customized knife and saw, he was well prepared to enjoy his time in the field. I never met the owner but I know him through his knife, a piece that speaks well of his knowledge and ability to transform a sharp tool into a better companion.

Conclusion:
We come to the world of knives by choice, not one person is held captive against their will. Freedom and dreams of knives, is what makes our time together so special. People from all walks of life bound together by a common interest, knives. There are as many trails in the world of knives as there are individuals, you are welcome to bring a friend.

Blades & the Social Milieu—Knives in School

When I was a little kid, my grandfather gave me my first pocketknife. It was a real Boy Scout knife. Well, actually it was marked "Boy Scout Knife." It wasn't the official Boy Scout knife because my grandfather could not afford one. It didn't matter. It was the best knife in the world to me. He gave it to me before I had enough strength in my hands to open the blades. As close as I can recall, I must have been in the second grade. I believe every boy in school had a pocketknife - or at least every boy I had anything to do with had a pocketknife. Come lunch time, weather permitting, we would gather on the city hall lawn and play mumbletypeg.

Gregory Scott (left), 7, and Christopher Scott, 6, hold their first forged knives with copper blades and deer-horn handles.

I remember the first time I sharpened a pencil with my pocketknife. This was much more important to me than learning where all those foreign countries were on the globe. It started a skill that I use daily. (I don't recollect the last time I looked at a globe.) I can't recall when I didn't carry a pocketknife. Without a pocketknife, I feel as nervous as bull calves at their first branding party.

I can't remember any kid cutting another kid at school. To even think about cutting or threatening to cut another kid would have been the worst social blunder we could commit. We carried knives because we had earned the trust of our parents, our peers and our teachers. To violate that trust in any way would have been an unpardonable sin. Any boy or girl who threatened to harm another kid with a knife would have been an absolute, total social outcast forever more!

Knives weren't weapons, they were tools. With a knife we could carve wood, clean and trim fingernails, dig out splinters, cut patches for bicycle tubes and core apples. I made a knife in school as part of a sixth-grade craft project. Knives weren't bad; they were a part of life then just like they are now. Trust was earned, trust was shared and we got along fine. The other day I heard a news program stating that kids would no longer be able to carry weapons to school. I didn't figure that was a big deal until I heard that pocketknives were considered weapons!

What kind of society is this? Carry a tool to school and you can be expelled. It doesn't matter what you are doing with the pocketknife, just that you have it is wrong?

Somehow our educators got off base. Now the whole system is out of whack. Why is it that we blame and punish all kids out of fear that one idiot may use a knife indiscriminately or threaten to do so? The problem is that the one low-life, despicable coward who would use the knife as a weapon will have one anyway. The rest of the student population is being punished for what someone else may do. The problem is that those in charge say that the pocketknife is the problem. Blame the pocketknife, not the child they insist. Then they punish all the children by depriving them of one of man's most universal tools.

What is this kind of reasoning costing us? By being subjected to such faulty philosophy, our children are learning some off-base reasoning that can only perpetuate itself later. When I was a kid, we all had pocketknives. We earned the right to carry a pocketknife and under no circumstances would we abuse that right. Along with the pocketknife, we learned something more important. We learned trust and responsibility, that we earned respect when we respected others.

Now the lesson is that the child isn't responsible. By taking the knife away, we take away one opportunity to earn trust, we take away one opportunity to be responsible. Pocketknives aren't hypothetical constructs, they are real life. Schools are supposed to teach our children how to make it in the real world. Where, outside of public schools and prisons, do you find the entire male population without pocketknives!

Schools are busy teaching all kinds of "important" things. Actually, most of that which is taught will never be important to the student once he leaves the school system. Seems like I remember a book called Schools Without Failure by Bill Glasser. In the book he claimed that over 80 percent of the time in school was wasted. Can't we spare a little time out of the school day to teach about tools and knives, and responsibility and respect?

The way I see it, somewhere around third grade, along with the Big Chief Tablet and crayons, there should be a pocketknife along the lines of the Boy Scout knife with a dull blade. The child's name would be engraved on the handle. Any transgression with that knife and he would be the only kid in school without a knife. Classroom discussion would be about responsibility, judgment, trust and a sense of community. If we went back to treating our children with respect and dignity we might find some Abe Lincolns in our future instead of the idiots who are running things now.

Somehow, somewhere along the line we, you and I, let this happen. I don't know how it happened; I don't even know if it can be corrected. I do know that anyone who figures pocketknives are weapons rather than tools can't be smart enough to prepare our children for life outside the public school system. It is time we start challenging the system that can set a policy such as this. With a little luck, maybe we can change the government and our educational system just enough that folks who dream up these kinds of ideas may be looking for a new job.

Copy: Is Imitation Really the Sincerest Form of Flattery?

When it comes to original works of art that don't readily lend themselves to exact duplication, can they be copied so that the two artists - the creator and the copier - share the same inspiration and pleasures, and create objects of equal form and beauty? I don't think so.

For art to extend beyond the artist or craftsman, its message must touch another. When a true appreciation of art (be it written, painted or handmade) is developed in any manner, two lifetimes of experience mesh, each with a varied composite of past experiences and expectations, to develop a single mindset, complicated even for the mutual pleasure of each individual.

Art comes in many forms. Be it a painting, knife, other object or thought, it is the catalyst that unites those involved. Charles Russell painted, drew and wrote his legacy for others to see. The art of William Scagel was produced with his hand, hammer, steel and fire. Both were true high achievers in their chosen fields and left you and I with much to appreciate.

Russell & Art

There can only be one Charles Russell. His art realistically preserved the West as it was, as he saw it and lived it. From the age of 16 he knew no other world. His drawings, paintings and sculptures and written word all spoke of his devotion to his love, the early Western way of life. He knew the existence, culture and time that he loved was passing. His art preserved that moment in the history of man and the prairie.

As with all great artists, many have stood alone for the sake of their art and clawed their way to the top. Their desire to explore and understand the realm that dominated their every thought made possible their ability to communicate their

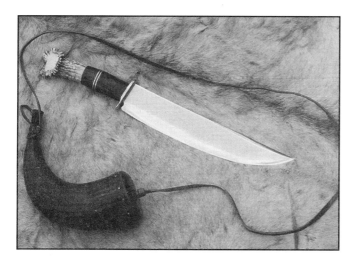

Wayne Goddard version of a Scagel - complete with a powder horn left behind by one of the last of Americas Great Free Buffalo Monarchs. All made by Wayne Goddard

vision. The honest message they wished to convey brings credibility to their art. These masters of their craft gave more to those who would listen and those who could see than they took from the world they loved. Their realistic art was a result of their experience, painstakingly developed abilities, and their devotion to the world they knew and understood so well.

The experience that leads to, and is gained from each creative work, is unique to that artist. Others can imitate a single thought or, rarely, a complete theme, but only one can feel, know and develop the full significance of the original. Some may be touched by many of the artist's works; others will feel the message from only one of many.

This is also the way it is in the world of knives. There can only be one true Excalibur, the blade of legend, though she is seen and heard each time by a different heart. Other elite blades, because of their unique qualities, stand alone at the top of their class. Each piece passes an elaborate dream from one person to another, even though they may be centuries or thousands of miles apart.

In the world of knives, several great makers have developed a truly unique art form. Every blade, from the first one each maker made, was the product of all their knowledge up to its completion. As their abilities and thoughts developed, all joined, each knife as a single, original event, the product of all that has come before and will meet the dream of tomorrow.

The differences in each work of art may be obscure to the casual observer, and can rarely be fully appreciated to a level that the creator of that work felt as his hand and heart developed his dream. All works of art are judged subjectively by one who appreciates, sees, feels and is touched by the message, bringing to bear another entire lifetime of experience.

William Scagel

William Scagel stands as the Charles Russell of the world of knives. Scagel used his blades and labored with his hands to create works of art that speak to many. Through his experiences, he developed his own artistic talents in many areas. While he is best known for his knives and understanding of knife function, he also created many other true works of art. He made Dutch ovens, magnificent beer steins, ornamental iron work and explored many areas of the blacksmith's art. He even made intricate braces for children crippled by polio, the design and function of which were a most giving kind of art to those who could not walk without them.

Scagel loved products of nature. He used natural materials to make individual statements of function and beauty. Steel, antler and leather intertwined to result in many individual rainbows from a true artist.

While all his blades cannot be appreciated by every hand and eye that explores them, each individual endeavor stands as a monument, an exclusive, individual contribution to the world of knives.

I own many books containing hundreds of photos and drawings of blades. Of the countless hours I have devoted to the study of the works of past and present makers, only a precious few send a message that touches me. While new realms of appreciation open each day, many knives known as champions to others seem to me devoid of creativity and function.

The characteristics that place some great blades above all others come from individuals who had the background, the imagination to see and the courage to dare travel where others have not been.

Many have tried to copy the outstanding accomplishments of the few who stand above all. Most fail for the simple reason that they cannot share the experiences that went into the development of the original art they try to copy. They did not make his first knife, they did not cut what he cut, see what he saw and feel what he felt. The copy always lacks the luster of the original unless, as some have done, the reproducer takes the time (and has the ability and devotion) to truly understand the total vision of the original maker, and then takes the knives to new levels by combining his experience with that of the original.

The copy is not without merit. Not all can afford or could ever have the opportunity to own the original. The artists who make the copies provide the opportunity for many to share a glimpse of some of the original masters' creativity.

While the copies cannot compete with the originals, they bring pleasure to many. They allow more individuals to share in some aspects of the masters' talent and the contribution of the man who, by virtue of his special gift of creativity, left the world of knives a better place.

Sweet Dreams Of Steel

Henry David Thoreau, one of the all-time-great authors and philosophers, had a tough time being recognized while he was alive. His first book was a failure as far as sales went. Out of 1,000 copies printed, 706 were returned to Thoreau unsold. Thoreau wrote, "I now have a library of nearly 900 volumes, over 700 of which I wrote myself. Is it not well that the author should behold the fruits of his labor?" Knifemaking is a lot like that for most makers.

There was a time when I had a collection of over 50 custom knives. All but one crude knife missing a handle and ground from a file with a broken tip were of my own making. I figured that I was rich—I owned the largest collection of Ed Fowler knives in existence! People thought I was nuts, what with my making knives like crazy, buying every old dying buck sheep with horns that I could afford and picking up dead-horned bucks and hauling them home just for getting the horns free. Sometimes my pick-up smelled like a slaughterhouse truck. It was ok though, because my dogs and the resident fox and coyotes all ate well, and I never wondered what to do with my spare time.

There's nothing easy about making knives for a living. The competition is tough. Each man has to develop his own market. Most makers have another source of income to support their knifemaking "habit." They have a full or part-time job, receive a pension or disability income, or their mates bring in a paycheck. When you start out, count on some hard times if your only income is from knives. You have to pay your dues, which means lots of disappointment and lots of opportunity. If you stick with it, you must be an eternal optimist.

The author bought every old dying buck sheep with horns that he could afford and hauled home dead-horned bucks to get the horns free.

Great knives can come from small, cluttered shops consisting of lots of used and homemade equipment. Here the author busies himself in his shop.

You've got to make knives because someone out there wants them—you hope!

There will be times when everyone around you will doubt that you can pull it off. I can't count the times I heard, "Why are you buying more buck sheep? You have enough horns!" or "What are you going to do with all of those knives?" When it comes right down to it, I made "all of those knives" for one reason and one reason only—because I wanted to! I am bored with television, don't require much sleep and am not prone to sit around and do nothing. I've got to do something, so why not make knives? Fact is, I eat, sleep, breathe and dream knives. It doesn't matter whether I am irrigating, branding or pulling a calf, likely as not a knife is on my mind. When I see a beautiful lady, I want to make a knife that looks and works like her. That is my dream—knives!

To be successful, makers must follow their dreams. Following a dream makes knifemaking easy. If your dream is to make lots of knives, sell them cheap and keep up a steady volume that is your dream—there's nothing wrong with that. Mass production is what made America great and mass-produced knives are what most knife buyers buy. The higher the goal you set for yourself when you start, the greater your achievements will be. Some wish only to make a few knives and please a few people. Others want to make knives that will be remembered by many. Some wish to help build an entire industry, while others are content to bring smiles to their corner of the world. Whatever your dream, it is yours and no one can take it away from you.

Great knives can come from small, cluttered shops consisting of lots of used and homemade equipment. Great knives can come from large, expensive shops with clean

You've got to make knives because someone out there wants them—you hope! Here Troy Christianson hammers steel to shape. (Christianson photo)

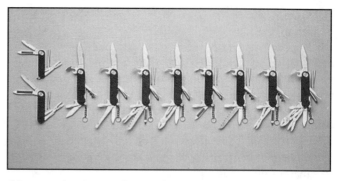

Mass production is what made America great and mass-produced knives—such as these Swiss Bucks are what most knife buyers buy.

floors and top-dollar equipment. For years my only power equipment was a well used 1/4-horsepower electric bench grinder and a hand-held electric drill. It took me hours to do what I can now do in minutes. I remember those days as good times. Remember: Dreamers know no bad times while they are following their dreams.

There are knife people who judge knives and makers by their dress. Such people will get what they pay for. Makers who have a real knife to sell do not need to worry about the style of knife they make, if the design is well thought out and it makes the statement of function or art that they wish to make. Great knives, like a great Christmas, come from the heart, not from the tinsel on the tree.

A maker needs to look at the so-called great knives of history, not so much to learn what to make but to avoid the mistakes of the past. Contrary to popular belief, most of the early pioneers made do with mass-production knives that were at best mediocre in design and function. When you see broken blades, deteriorated or missing handles and worn-out sheaths, the makers of the past are talking to you. Many makers make knives early in their careers that they will be repairing during their retirement years. Well-thought-out designs and materials will be worthwhile in the long run. There are a lot of experts on knives. They always know what you should make and where you should sell it. They have all sorts of ideas and their word is all powerful. They tell the knife collector whose knives to collect and they tell the maker what kind of knife to make. Don't listen to them. Dream your dream, make knives to fill that dream and your success will be forthcoming. Tradition is important to some and that is ok, non-dreamers need stability. Just don't be afraid to dream and test your dream in the marketplace.

A New Dress for Lady Knife

I knew it the moment I entered the front door. The gun shop was different somehow; a warm glow illuminated the back of it. Normal sounds were different, conversation had a different tone, the coffee smelled sweeter. An event of true consequence was about to make its mark on history.

This is how she looked when I brought her home. She was rusted, had a mushroomed back, and a crudely ground hollow grind. She had been through a lot.

Walking to the showcase where I go weekly to see what pieces of antiquity have been dug out of the woodwork, I saw one of those fine old knives that I knew I would never forget. It doesn't happen often but, for a few, precious moments, time stopped. I stared and she just kind of laid there and stared back at me. Nothing else existed for those moments known only to true knife lovers.

She wasn't any lady of virtue, she was one of those high-mileage models that had been rode hard and put away wet. Her back had been hammered with something big, heavy and hard. She was mushroomed so bad that she had trouble getting in and out of her sheath. Her sides had been ground on a wheel so coarse you got lost trying to look her over from guard to tip. Someone's idea of a good time had scarred her terribly. Her back was bent and rust had left its sad scar. I wasn't bothered by the fact that she had been around. I have known lots of ladies like her. I knew that with a little time and patience I could bring her back to the lady she once could have been.

Her style and marks proclaimed her a U.S. Model 1917 C.T. Bolo. made by Fayette R. Plumb, St, Louis, 1918. Her scabbard had been with her throughout her life, stamped "A-

K CO. 1918 R.H.S." I had heard stories about her. Some claimed her to be an angel of cut, a welcome friend to any man's hand. Others claimed that she wasn't worth having, calling her too heavy, too hard or too soft. I wanted to know for myself. They wanted $20 for her pleasures. I offered $5. Several days went by and for $10 she was mine to hold, straighten, grind and polish till another lady pulls us apart.

My first thoughts were to test the blade for hardness, do a little regrinding and test the cutting ability. I found that she was rather soft, having been hardened uniformly from back to edge, guard to tip. She cut pretty well but her edge geometry left a lot to be desired. After several hours on the belt grinder, she cut quite a bit better. I thought about stripping her down, putting her in the forge and doing some serious remanufacturing. I decided that I would enjoy her more by leaving her basic nature as she was, and limited my endeavors to cleaning her up like I wanted her to be. I left her back like it was, just cleaned up the mushrooming so she could fit her scabbard without tearing it up. I didn't try to reharden her, just took the bends out of her back and gave her a clean, efficient cutting edge.

Some of you non-believers may accuse me of anthropomorphism, but that is what makes knifemakers like me—knives are friends, companions, have personalities and provide a lot of memories.

This is the way she looked when I had done all I wanted. The handles and guard are left the way they were. I just added some oil and cleaned up the rust. The ricasso blends the way she was with the way she is: clean and honest. She will shave hair but doesn't win any edge-holding contests.

A Knife for Mom

(Above) The author's greatgrandmother, who lived in the latter part of the 18th century probably around the time that the knife was made. Fruit knives usually had blades of silver or gold for corrosion resistance at a time when stainless steel was unavailable. Men gave fruit knives as presents to their wives or girlfriends. According to Bill Karsten's book, "Silver Folding Fruit Knives, "

This fine old silver fruit knife with the intricately pinned pearl handle came to me in a trade. I accepted it with the intention of getting my investment out of it as soon as possible. Then I noticed the inscription, "Mother." Time and time again I picked up the knife, looking it over and over, each time returning to the inscription. I have tried to envision the artist who made this elegant tribute to mother, and I have wondered about the moms who have cherished this knife down through the years.

I tried to make lots of things for my mother. When I was a kid I made the things that kids make: I drew pictures, decorated her curtains and walls with crayons, maybe even stitched up a pot holder or two. Whatever it was she always liked it, except some chocolate-covered grasshoppers that didn't go over too big. Or was it ants?

I made her some knives, the kind I felt she could use around the kitchen. She always talked them up and was real appreciative (she used them as much as she could) then she would see another one that I made that she liked better and would ask if she could trade. Looking back I feel kind of sorry for her, trying to use in the kitchen the kinds of knives that I made. Most of what I know about kitchens comes from watching someone else do it.

This silver fruit knife was and is perfect. No mother could want any more. It is delicate, beautiful and radiates the ideal tribute to the ideal mother. The tip has a little twist in it, probably due to some son or grandson trying to use it as a screwdriver. I don't believe that his mother was too unhappy about the damage—she probably cherished the scar on the blade tip as much as the knife itself. But that's a mother for you: we mess up and she puts it in her scrapbook.

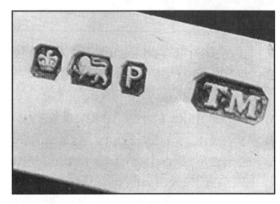

The word "Mother" was frequently engraved on fruit knives.

The hallmarks on the blade of the author's silver fruit knife reveal the following, from left: the crown means the knife was made in Sheffield; the lion passant indicates the knife blade is silver; the P means the knife was made in 1907; and TM is the initials for the maker. Thomas Marples was the most famous TM and was making fruit knives as early as the mid-19th century. However, the absence of the Queen Victoria hallmark on the blade means the knife was made sometime after 1890. This TM probably indicates the knife was made in the Marple's shop after Marples' death.

A Knifemaker's Best Christmas Present

I still remember the first time I was honored to share another's Christmas Day, even though I was miles away. One of my knives was under his family's Christmas tree. That morning I was more excited about the events taking place far away than the Christmas at my own home. Days before I had been walking around with a smile on my face in expectation of the vicarious honor I would feel participating in another's Christmas through the product of my labor and experience. At times I was apprehensive: what if he didn't like it? Then my optimistic outlook on life would take over. Heck, he had to like it, I did!

I had visions of the small package under the tree patiently waiting the opening of presents. Would it be opened first or last? What if it got lost? Did they open their presents Christmas Eve or Christmas morning. The pressure was unbearable.

Christmas day finally came and I hadn't heard anything. Minutes became hours and still no news. Finally noon came and I couldn't wait any longer—I called him. How did he like it? What did he say? The knife was a hit! I then returned to my own time and place.

Over the years I have had the privilege of sharing Christmas with other families through my knives. Wives and mothers have carefully picked among the knives that I had to offer. Some were confident that their choice would be the correct one for their special man; others were concerned about his being able to trade the knife for another should their choice be the wrong one. No matter how many times the event repeats itself, I always feel a sense of extreme honor and well-being when one of my knives is chosen as a present for a loved one.

Knives find their way into many different homes and lifestyles. The gal who runs the feed store, the cattle buyer and the fur trader. The doctor who takes care of my children. The son of my insurance agent. The veterinarians who care for our animals. The rancher who puts his knives through the same kind of torture that I do, the trapper, the guide and the Boy Scout leader. Then there are the many more whom I have met only once, and the more yet whom I have met through the mail or on the phone. Coming from all tax brackets and areas of the country, they have allowed me to share in their lives through my knives.

Christmas for a knifemaker starts months in advance of Dec. 25. Completing knives that were promised for The Big Day always places pressure on the knifemaker. I tend to worry a lot more about injuries I could suffer around the ranch at that time of year because it might prevent me from making knives and cause me to let someone down on their expectations for Christmas.

Second only to Christmas itself comes the joy of seeing and hearing about the use of my knives. I have given 'special deals' to those who couldn't afford them, simply because I felt that I had received more pleasure from seeing the knife go to a good home than the money could have meant.

Each Christmas I tell myself that next year I will have more knives immediately available. And due to the drive generated by the Christmas spirit, I can usually be found on Christmas Day in my shop, making knives.

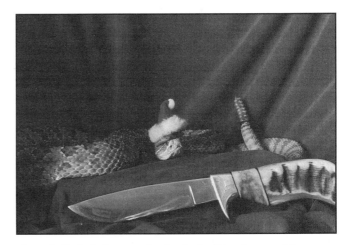

Santa's little helper rattles in the holiday by watching over one of Ed's pronghorn knives!

Snake Steak: How to Skin a Rattler!

The Blade *Editor's Caution To The Reader. You will notice that the following story tells you how to skin a rattler but not how to kill one. That's because venomous snakes are deadly animals and "Blade" magazine is not in the business of telling you how to end the life of a creature that could do the same to you.*

This is meant to be a fun article but it does have an extremely serious side. I was bitten by a rattler once. It was an interesting experience. I came very close to death and six months later I'm still not completely over it. The hospital bill was in the neighborhood of $7,000 and medications since that time haven't been cheap.

Snakes are extremely quick. Avert your eyes for a moment and they will be on you in an instant. You would not believe how easy a snake's bite will sink into your skin. It's like your skin has zero resistance to those fangs. There is no such thing as a dead venomous snake until the head is cut from the body and has been properly disposed of in such a manner that no kid or animal can get hold of the business part of said snake.

Years ago a friend was going to cut the rattles off a "dead" prairie rattler for a souvenir. He was warned to cut the head off the rattler before removing the rattles. He laughed it off but our warning kept coming until finally he lopped off the head before removing the rattles. He made a big show of stepping on the snake's neck and cutting off the head with a pocketknife. He turned and asked "is the snake 'dead' enough yet?", claiming that we were a bunch of overcautious sissies. He picked up the snake, that was now wiggling some, and proceeded to cut the rattles free.

As soon as the knife bit into the tail section of the rattler, the headless snake wound around and smacked my friend in the wrist with a bloody stump of a neck. My friend yelled, we laughed and then he passed out, hitting the ground like a goner. He was so long in coming to that we wondered if he ever was going to come around. When he did, he wasn't in any mood to take a teasing and since he was a lot bigger than any of us, we didn't say too much. I could relate a lot of "dead" snake stories but you probably get my drift. Safety first! Getting bit is serious business.

I like rattlers. I do not advocate killing them indiscriminately. I realize that confrontations between snake and man happen. Snakes can be in the wrong place and when this happens the snake is most likely to lose its life. I hate to see any one of God's creatures go to waste. But if you have to kill it, the rattler has one of the most beautiful skins and some good tasting meat.

How To Do It

Author's note: Pete Petty is my friend. He is a local legend. Pete knows rattlers better than anyone else I know. He

1. Cut the hide on the belly just ahead of the rattles and work toward where the head was before you cut it off

2. Continue splitting the skin, in the center of the belly, working toward the neck.

traps them, catches them, sells them, skins and eats them. Pete has skinned more rattlers than most men will ever see. He is one of those few individuals who will sit and talk rattlers for hours on end and never repeat himself. Pete spent a lot of time teaching me about handling rattlers and has shared his knowledge without reservation. Following is Pete's method of skinning a rattler and getting it ready for the pot":

Skinning a rattler is easy. Start at the rattles and cut in the center of the belly, working your way up to the vent (the cloaca, or where the intestinal, urinary and generative canals discharge). Cut the vent free from the skin and continue on up to the neck. Work the skin loose around the neck, it is easy to tear the skin in this area, then peel the skin down to the rattles. Cut the rattles and skin loose from the body. Salt the skin and roll it up. It will keep for a few days until you can get it to a taxidermist or you can tan it yourself by soaking it in Pre-

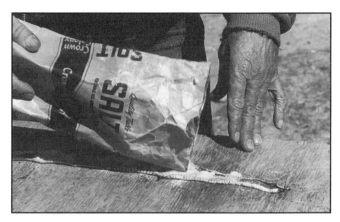

5. Spread the hide out and salt it down. You can use table salt or whatever is handy, as long as it is good old sodium chloride.

3. Once you split the hide from the rattles to the neck, work the hide loose around the neck and peel the skin off, just like peeling a banana.

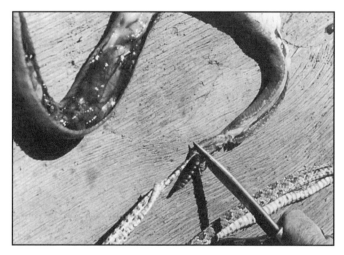

6. Work the salt in and roll the skin up till you can get it to your tanning solution.

4. Peel from the neck all the way down to the rattles. Be careful here or you may have to glue the rattles back on to the skin. Carefully skin to the rattles, then cut the rattles free from the snake's body.

stone© or glycerine and alcohol. If you need to flesh the skin, remember to flesh toward the head to avoid cutting through the skin.

Cooking the meat is easy. Any recipe for chicken or fish will work for rattlesnake meat, or try this recipe if you like:

7. Cleaning a snake is easier than cleaning a fish. Grab hold and pull from neck to tail and you're done.

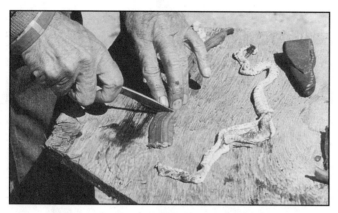

9. Here it is: a belt and a meal on its way to happening.

8. Cut the body into pan-size pieces. Care here keeps the sharp pieces of bone to a minimum.

Skin snake and cut meat into 3- to 4inch pieces. Roll meat in mixture of flour, cornmeal, milk and egg. Salt and pepper. Deep fry in hot oil. Serve hot. Rattlers have lots of bones and I hate to try to eat them when I'm real hungry; it seems like you will starve to death before getting to the meat around the bones.

Epilogue to *Snake Steak*:

Pete Petty was my friend we shared a lot of time about rattlers. He had been bitten several times and continued to caution me when I became too familiar with them, telling me I would get bit one day. When I got bit it was a good one, scoring over $7,000 worth of hospital bills. Pete was the one person who understood why I had to get bit. It was an opportunity to share a little more of nature than most like. The experience was and continues to be very impressive. While in the hospital during the critical stage after the bite, I saw the other side and learned that it is a pretty nice place to be. I do not recommend this kind of curiosity to anyone else as it definitely is hazardous to your health. Pete died soon after this article appeared in *Blade*. He was a good man, lived well in nature and is missed.

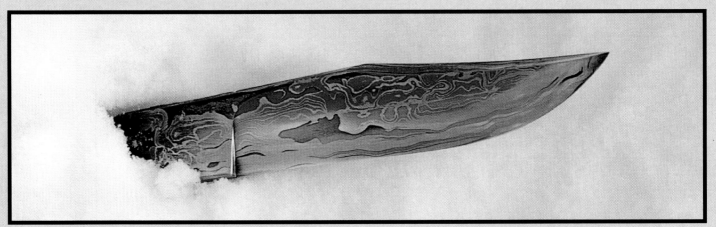

Damascus blade in snow. (Fowler)

The 90° flex test. (Fowler)

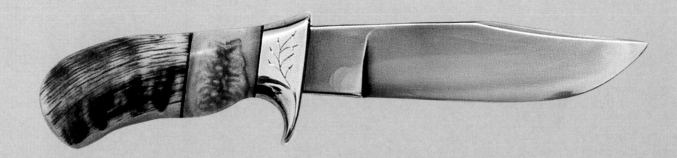

Some of Fowler's various Bowies. (Fowler)

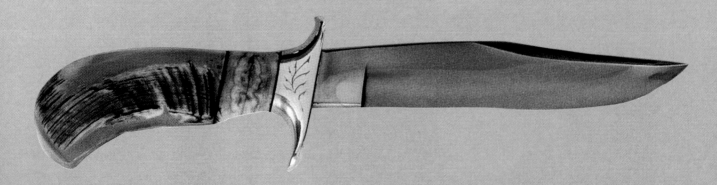

Fowler Camp Knives.

Large Camp Knife: blade 10-1/4"; handle 5-1/2". (Barry Gallagher photo)

Long Pronghorn. (Barry Gallagher Photo)

The classic Pronghorn with a handstitched sheath made of waxed harness leather.
The sheath is custom made for the knife. (Barry Gallagher Photo)

The blades of the master smith. These were Ed's test blades for his master smith status.
(Barry Gallagher photo)

Pronghorn. Notice the knife's temper lines. (Barry Gallagher photo)

Pronghorn Knife. (Barry Gallagher photo)

All above photos - Pronghorn. (Fowler)

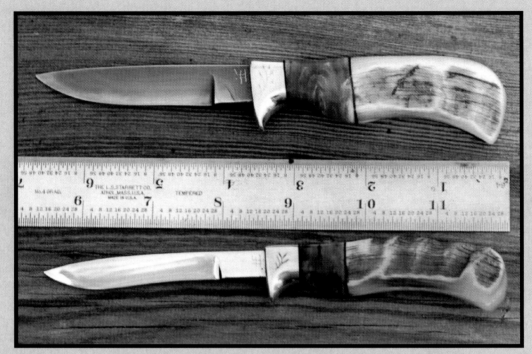

Fowler's Bird and Trout model. (Fowler)

Bowie knife: blade 8"; handle 5". (Barry Gallagher photo)

The Knifemaker Time Almost Forgot

Every spring there is a doubleheader gun and antique show in Riverton, Wyoming. This year's show brought me face-to-face with the knives of an unknown maker that would carry his message over 30 years after his death.

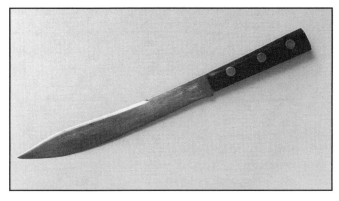

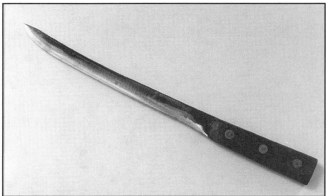

The author says Berry's knives are made with function in mind.

Dennis Knopik and his wife, Anne, are antique dealers and my good friends. In the past 20 years we have spent some good times talking antiques at the show. Several times he mentioned having some custom knives made by George I. Berry. Dennis had learned about Berry after buying some items from the Wilda Berry estate. Berry was daughter of George Berry. The knives and an article in the Jan. 21, 1940, edition of *The Casper Tribune Herald* of Casper, Wyoming, were in an old trunk that the Knopiks had bought from the estate.

It seems like I spend a lot of time listening to how someone's brother, uncle or grandfather used to make knives. Most of the time I am greatly interested and ask a lot of questions. I am especially interested in the various heat-treating methods.

When Dennis started telling me about Berry's knives, I wasn't too impressed. Dennis said that Berry had "cold forged the blades to harden them" and that he made a lot knives out of the steel from automobile fenders. Everybody knows that car fenders don't make good knives. That's a rule. Ask any knifemaker about cold forged knives from low carbon steel and he will smile and change the subject.

Dennis showed me one of Berry's knives. The knife appeared to be well made. The edge geometry was better than most and the knife was definitely made with function in mind. As I studied it I began to take Berry's work more seriously. Dennis asked me to test one of the knives. That same day I found another of Berry's pieces for sale at A.J. White's Buffalo Trading Post in Shoshonie. The knife had been rode hard and put away wet. I took it to my shop, sharpened it and proceeded to test it.

The edge flexed over a steel without chipping, indicating that the blade was not too hard. I resharpened the blade and cut some rope. I was surprised —80 cuts! Six more cutting trials provided consistent results. Berry's cold-forged, low-carbon-steel blade consistently out performed a lot of the best knives made today!

I asked Dennis if I could take a closer look at the Jan. 21, 1940, *Casper Tribune Herald* that accompanied the Berry knives in the estate sale. On the front page there's a story about Winston Churchill urging all nations to join Britain and France against Nazi Germany, warning that all Europe faces war. On page 12 appears the best remaining information on the knives of George I. Berry.

The article is fascinating. Berry lived in Casper. He was injured, leaving his left hand crippled, yet nonetheless started making knives. One of his favorite pieces was a knife-and-fork design that enabled a one-handed man to cut and eat with one hand. The story quoted him as saying that knives didn't need too much carbon, and that he liked steel with as little as .2 percent carbon for his blades. He also made knives out of spring steel and field hatchets out of grader blades. He was particularly proud of his design for a pancake turner that would fit either a round pan or a square one with a 'twist of the wrist." Unfortunately, the story writer didn't ask the right questions for me to know how Berry worked the steel.

As far as I can tell, this fascinating, forgotten knifemaker died sometime in the late 1940s. He left an interesting story and some fine knives behind. He made a good knife. He made his own rivets, using copper wire or brass most of the time. He didn't sign any that I've seen, but his workmanship is fairly distinctive, especially when you have a little history to go along with the knife. Dennis said he had never seen a signature on any of the knives either, but that Berry's workmanship stands out enough to make identifying his knives possible.

This old Berry hatchet sports steel from a road grader. Though the author says its edge geometry is not as good as other Berry pieces, it still does the job.

Without doing sophisticated, destructive tests on his blades, it's hard to tell exactly how Berry made knives as well as he did. The important thing to remember is that he was able to make high-performance blades over 40 years ago, using steel and methods that we would consider inferior today.

Obviously, performance was important to him, and he was able to make a superior knife. His work tells me that there is much to be learned when it comes to making high-performance blades. Next time someone tells me that his great uncle made great knives out of ant dust and marshmallows, I will take him seriously.

The Best Knifemaker Nobody Remembers

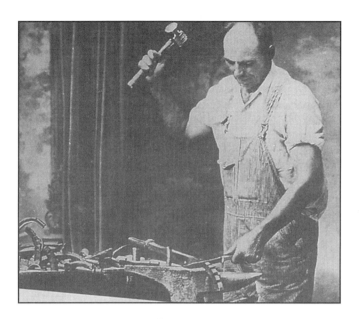

The original photo of Frank Richtig that was reproduced in cartoon form (below) by Ripley's Believe It or Not ®.

"I first became acquainted with custom knives and Richtig sometime in the 1950s while reading the Sunday paper. He was pictured in Ripley's Believe It Or Not ® *cutting a buggy axle with one of his knives."* (© *1994 Ripley Entertainment Inc., Registered Trademark of Ripley Entertainment Inc.®*)

Great functional knives have stood the test of time. The knives of Frank J. Richtig have passed that test. Not only did he build a piece that was years ahead of its time, he promoted his product with honestly, ingenuity and determination to such an extent that his knives became widely known at a time when most custom knifemakers worked in obscurity. He did all that was necessary and he did it on his own, leaving the world with a better knife, and knifemakers with a goal for which to strive.

Richtig was born Dec. 28, 1887. He passed away Jan. 28, 1977, at age 89. His knifemaking career spanned 50 years, from 1926 to 1976. He made knives that were plain and easily affordable by most households. He made some very nice custom hunting and fishing knives, as well as some elegant Bowies. All of his knives had one thing in common: Those he made 66 years ago will outperform most of the knives made today.

I first became acquainted with custom knives and Richtig sometime in the 1950s while reading the Sunday paper. He was pictured in "Ripley's Believe It Or Not" cutting a buggy axle with one of his knives. I am told that the story first appeared sometime in 1938, a year before I was born.

Several years ago I met maker Harlan Suedmeier at the Oregon Knife Collectors Association Show in Eugene, Oregon. Harlan was displaying some of Richtig's knives. I had always wanted to examine a Richtig knife and Harlan not

only allowed me to examine them, he spent a great deal of time sharing information about the knives and the man who made them. We discussed the possibility of my borrowing some of the knives to test them. Harlan was more than willing to help me with the project.

He supplied me with a number of knives that Richtig had made at different times in his career, and asked that I give them a fair test and let him know the results. I sharpened the knives and spent several days using them, doing what knives are supposed to do - cut. It didn't take long to realize that I was using knives that had been made by a man who had definitely soared with the eagles. Not only did his knives cut better than 99 percent of those that I have ever tested, the handles were comfortable and the overall design was more than acceptable.

Suedmeier stopped by my shop to watch and I asked him what he thought about putting one of the knives through a complete performance test. Harlan was not only willing but enthusiastically encouraged me to test one of the knives any way that I felt would contribute to an accurate evaluation. We selected a thin-blade, well-used kitchen knife. I sharpened it and proceeded to cut a free-hanging, 1-inch hemp rope. The knife was a lot lighter than most knives that are able to pass the test but it still sliced a piece of the rope easily. I then cut a two-by-four pine board in half twice and the blade still cut hair.

I was reluctant to subject a knife that could never be replaced to a 90˚ flex test, but again Harlan assured me that he wanted a complete test performed. I placed the tip of the blade in a vice and flexed the blade to 90'. The blade did not chip or crack and I returned it to within five degrees of straight.

Most of the knives made today cannot come close to this level of performance. Richtig obviously had developed heat treating methods that allowed him to get the most out of his steel. He was an outstanding knifemaker. He did all that was necessary to be included in the circle of "elite" knifemakers. He developed a superior product, promoted it with skill and ingenuity, and supplied his community with an honest knife that was—and still is—a cut above the rest.

Heroes

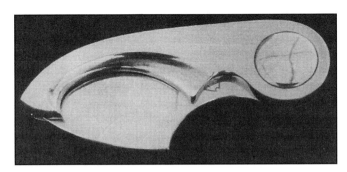

Ray Appleton names all his knives and the name he chose for the one he made for Martin was, appropriately enough, "Love Ya."

We all have heroes. Sometimes our heroes are what we thought they would be; sometimes they are only what we wished they would be. I'm lucky. My hero is still a hero 45 years after I first met him. Ray Appleton was my hero when I was 10 years old. He had the fastest car, the best dog and the prettiest lady of anyone I knew. Ray stood taller than anyone else and, no matter what, always had a smile and friendly "hello." He could out ski anyone on the ski slope, fix anything that was broken and make anything that was worth making.

Now I'm in my 50s and Ray is still my hero. We lost track of each other for over 35 years until I talked to him at a Blade Show when it was in Knoxville, Tennessee. Though I suspected it, at the time I didn't know he was the same Ray Appleton of my childhood. I thought about it for days and decided that it just had to be him. I wrote him a letter and, a few days later, he called. My hero and I knew each other again.

Ray makes knives that transcend other knives. They are the artwork of a mechanical genius. He doesn't turn out hundreds of knives, just a few, very special, one-of-a-kind pieces that you can recognize as his work from across the room. Every Appleton knife represents a lot of labor and a lifetime of experience and imagination backed by the knowledge of a true master of his craft. Special blades attract special admirers and, sometimes, strong bonds form between the maker and client. The following events portray one of those special relationships that makes true heroes and great knives what they are—dependable.

Martin

Rich and poor, young and old, male and female, we all come together to share knife experiences. The times shared are good. As a result of these encounters, friendships are forged that span barriers that normally would keep us apart. Knives are gifts that transcend the barriers of prejudice, hatred and language. Blades also easily bridge the age barrier.

Father and son, grandfather and grandchild can all talk freely in the world of knives. When the barrier breaks and communication starts, the talk begins about blades and often extends beyond them. Many times, matters of true consequence can be shared and felt forever.

All parents fear the loss of a child and pray that the youngest in the family will be the last to die. The loss of a child hurts. I know of no pain that lasts and gnaws and eats on a parent quite like it. This is one pain that doesn't go away; it just stays and stays. It eats on our thoughts and dominates your mind until you accept that it will always be with you, and you walk with the pain as your companion forever.

Once in a great while, mutual interest, guided by destiny, brings people together to share some of the extreme joys and sorrows that are a part of living. When you touch those who grieve, you touch all who love. All who hear and know would

Martin performed all sorts of odd jobs around the hospital to "pay" for his Appleton knife.

do anything to ease the pain of those who have lost a loved one. The good times are easy; the worst times can bring out the best of those trapped in the events taking place. The pain of a lost loved one can seem unbearable. However, along with that pain comes an awareness that, through the sharing of the hardship, we all come a little closer to understanding what love is all about. Martin was a super-sharp 8-year-old. His enthusiasm, quest for knowledge and love of life made sharing time with him a joy.

Martin loved knives. He had begun a blade collection and wanted to know more about knives. Like every blade lover, Martin spent a lot of time reading about knives. Martin's father bought him a copy of one of the better blade books available, the third edition of *Levine's Guide To Knives And Their Values.*

Out of the thousands of blades described in Bernard Levine's book, Martin found some special pieces that he liked. On page 289 of the book, four Ray Appleton knives are fea-

Appleton said 8-year-old Martin's understanding of life and death was far beyond that of other boys his age.

tured. Nowhere are there any blades that look like Appleton's. He is one of the most innovative, original and magnificent knifemakers of our time. His pieces stand alone as ultimate precision works of art. Due to their beauty and complexity, his folders are, in all probability, the most sought-after of all handmade folding knives.

The price of the Appleton knives pictured in Levine's book ranged from $3,000 to $11,000. The price didn't hold Martin back. As blade enthusiasts, we all know that once a craftsman sends a message that we hear, we will pursue the knife in any way possible. Be it only to see or touch it or talk about it for a time, we will get as close to it as we can. Martin was in love as only another knife enthusiast can understand.

The quest for Martin's Appleton knife had begun. Martin could not afford one of Ray's pieces, but talking to the maker, or possibly even getting a photo of one of them, would be a moment to remember for him. Martin's dad called Bernard Levine wanting to know how to contact Ray. Levine gave him Appleton's phone number and address and a storybook relationship was about to begin.

Martin and Ray

Martin called Ray. They talked knives and quickly became friends. Then, Ray talked to Martin's father. The father told Ray what Ray already knew - that Martin was a special kind of boy. Problem was, Martin didn't have much time left. He had leukemia and, in all probability, would not live to see an Appleton knife in person. He was going into the hospital for chemotherapy and, even with treatment, the prognosis for Martin was grave.

During Ray's and Martin's friendship, most of Martin's time was spent in the hospital. During his hospital stay, he was allowed to use the phone for personal use. The long-distance calls to Ray were paid for by the good wishes of all who came in contact with Martin. As Ray and Martin talked, they became good friends - and more. They talked about life and death, of heaven and earth, and their friendship grew out of mutual respect shared by two friends who knew their time was limited.

Martin had some odd jobs at the hospital. He earned money by reading and telling stories to other children who were also hospitalized. Martin's positive attitude and enthusiasm were an inspiration to other children who were also trapped in bodies that required serious treatment. Martin was saving the money he made in order to pay for his Appleton knife.

Ray made Martin his dream knife and, when Martin's time on earth came to an end, his Appleton knife was in his hand. Martin's wish was that the knife be with him always. Martin's ashes were spread upon the ice of a frozen lake. His father dropped the Appleton knife through a hole drilled in the ice to await the spring thaw when the boy and his knife would be together in the waters that have cleansed, nourished and bound all life for all time.

Epilogue

The story doesn't end there. While Martin wanted his own Appleton knife, he also wanted a lasting gift for his father. Ray received in the mail Martin's private knife collection, a carved bear that had been among Martin's most cherished possessions, and the money Martin had saved from his job at the hospital. The money was not in payment for his knife - that Martin knew was a gift from Ray - but as payment for an Appleton knife as a gift from Martin to his father. The carved bear, some special knives from a true friend's collection and many memories have since become Ray's most prized possessions.

The Day I Met Bob Loveless

Bob Loveless (Weyer photo)

One aspect of knife shows that always intrigues me is getting to know the individuals who attend. Some walk through a show and only look at the surface, while others walk slowly from table to table and see all there is to see.

I've tried to explore the vision of those who carefully inspect the knives at each table by asking what they see. Only rarely do I get a glimpse into their thoughts. Nonetheless, I still know that even the most minute detail comes to their attention. It matters little whether or not they buy a knife. I consider it an honor to share time with them through the experience of common visions about blades.

The first major show I attended was one of Dan Delavan's California Custom Knife shows. I was a rank newcomer to the world of knives. As I walked through the show, I saw Bob Loveless sitting behind a table of blades. I wanted to in-

troduce myself, but was too much in awe of his art and reputation in the world of knives.

Twice I approached his table and each time failed to initiate any conversation. I have regretted this weakness on my part as the years have passed. I was delighted to learn that I was to get a reprieve when Steve Shackleford told me that Loveless was going to share some knife talk with those at the banquet the Saturday night of the California Custom Knife Show this past fall.

Bob and I met during the show. This time I made it a point to introduce myself and shake his hand. His smile and greeting welcomed me. Then, while he was sitting at the table next to mine autographing copies of Jim Weyer's excellent photographic history of his knives, *Living on the Edge: Logos of the Loveless Legend* (from which the accompanying photos are excerpted), our converstation naturally drifted to blades and steel. I found him to be well informed, a man of true vision and deserving of his place as a leader in the world of knives.

Though Loveless is known for his expertise as a stock-removal artist and I'm a dedicated hammer-and-anvil man, there was no friction between us. As we talked, I found that we shared similar thoughts concerning our love of knives, art and steel. Through our conversation it became evident that we each faced the same opportunities and traveled parallel paths-though using differing methods each seeking the best knife we could make. While our approaches are a little different, our goals are the same, so our common interest unified the conversation.

Loveless is one of the pioneers in the frontiers of the custom knife. He started with the dream of his own Iron Mistress and stuck with her when the going got tough. Through his dedication, commitment and ability he has provided many the opportunity to enjoy one more beauty in the world of blades. Part of the respect and degree of excellence that the custom knife has earned is owed to men like him who provide inspiration to all blade enthusiasts. His influence will continue to make the world of knives a better place for a long time to come.

If you want to know, don't be bashful. Whether it's Loveless, Appleton, Jay Hendrickson, or whoever, introduce yourself and talk blades. Chances are, you'll be welcome. There need be no strangers in the world of knives. Sharing is what blades are all about.

Reflections On Steel

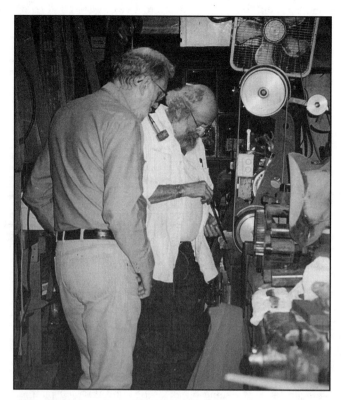

"Through the years there were some great teachers and friends who shared their experiences and abilities with me, carefully sending me down the road, each time walking a little straighter," the author writes. Here he shares some grinding tips with Dr. James Lucie. (Fowler photo)

As I write these words, I am preparing for a knife show. The more I look over the knives that I am taking to the show, the better I feel. These are some great knives. Each year brings new ways of doing things and subtle changes that only the most serious student of my knives will ever be able to detect.

It seems like many years ago that I had taken a couple of classes on knifemaking. I was just getting started making knives seriously. At that time I felt that I knew all there was to know about making knives. Granted, I had made a lot of progress in a short time, but little did I know how much more there was to learn. There was a time when new knowledge and techniques resulted in significant changes in the performance or appearance of my knives. Today's changes are more subtle yet still bring me great pleasure as I make them.

There was a time when I felt knifemaking was pretty simple and that I would be able to continue making knives until the last days of my life should I live to see that magic 100-year mark. I now know that while it is possible to make knives for quite awhile, a few injuries and events are telling

me that making knives isn't as simple nor will I be able to make them for as long as I once thought I could.

While it is possible to make usable knives without putting too much sophisticated technique into them, a man is limited to the time he has to make his top-of-the-line effort. Like life, it is a full circle. The top is a matter of degree, not miles; just a little better, then ease on down the other side of the hill.

Another thing that I spend a lot of time thinking about is that many things influence a knifemaker's career. Some of them are influenced by him, and some of them just kind of happen independently, then come together to result in something that is far greater than the sum of its parts. Take me for example. When I was about 4 years old, my father promised me a knife but didn't deliver on his promise. That incident instilled in me a thirst for knives that continues to grow.

The author said he is thankful for the good will, good times, the smiles and fond memories he has shared through his association with knives. Here he (left) presents one of Blade magazine's Knife-of-the-Year Awards at the 1994 Blade Show Banquet.

My grandfather was raised in an orphanage, so as a kid he had to make anything that he wanted, or he didn't get it. He taught me how to make everything from rabbit traps to wooden swords and knives out of pieces of lath. He showed me how to use a hand-powered grinder that I used to finish the knives. I traded these first "custom knives" for comic books. Later, he gave me my first real knife and taught me how to use and care for it. He was a superior craftsman and artist, as well as a preacher with lots of love and faith. His guidance started me off with a sincere and deep appreciation for all quality handmade products, and those who are able to create them at an early age.

Through the years there were some great teachers and friends who shared their experiences and abilities with me, carefully sending me down the road, each time walking a little straighter. One boss I especially remember explained that he would teach me how to do the job and from that time on quality was my responsibility, that it was my name that was going on it and if it was done right, I would be the one to benefit. That conversation took place over 30 years ago and I still remember his words like it was yesterday.

Events that occurred at my first major knife show set the table for everything that has followed. The show was Dan Delavan's California Custom Knife Show in Anaheim, California . I met some of the knife industry's top people, including writer Gary Kelley . We talked and he took some pictures of me and my knives. One of those pictures of me smiling and holding a knife appeared in Blade magazine. The caption under the photo referred to my gnarled hands and that I had a "heart as big as all outdoors."

Those words introduced me to more people than I had met in my first 40 years. Those words set an expectation in the minds of the people I meet and are a constant reminder to me. I know that I am responsible to my customers as well as others in the world of knives to make the best knife that I can make, but even more important than that are the good will, the good times, smiles and fond memories. Thanks to all that has gone into making me what I am, someone who feels privileged to share with those who do me the honor of letting me into their lives as a friend.

What is a knife show? A knife show is an opportunity for friends old and new to meet and share good times about knives. A knife show is a place where a lot more comes together than the eye can see; it's where each man, woman and child brings a lifetime of experiences, as well as hopes and dreams of the future, together for good times and knives.

Welcome To The Big Dance

Vested interest Ed Landy wore his favorite pastime like a badge at the Blade Show

The Blade Show & International Cutlery Fair in Atlanta, Georgia, is where everything comes together, from the planning, making of knives and the long hours getting ready for the show until the final sleep before the flight to the show begins.

When you start from a long way off like I do (Wyoming), the day usually starts way before breakfast. Angela and I started early and, as we left home, our plane flew into the sunrise surrounded by brilliant red clouds. The Blade Show was seven hours, two airports and a taxi ride away. Even after all the shows I have attended, my excitement is still the same; it starts to build months before the show and just keeps getting better.

Scores of knifemakers, knife collectors, knife writers, knife suppliers, those who make grinders and cases, the engravers and scrimshanders, the photographers and editors from all the major knife publications, and others from all over the world, each from a different way of life, were bringing their own individual contribution to this gathering of the world of knives. All were beginning their journey to the same place, the Greatest Knife Show in the World, the Blade Show.

Meeting in Atlanta would be the old timers and legends who have contributed, unselfishly grooming the world of knives to make it the place of friendship, beauty and function that it is. The newcomers also would visit the show, some of whom will enter the world of knives for a short time and then move on to something else, as well as those fresh faces who will stay, each enriching the blade world by their experience and dedication.

There would be the nervous journeyman and master smith applicants coming to the show and their introduction to the American Bladesmith Society. Among the journeyman candidates were my friends, Josh Smith and Audra Draper. Thinking about their nervousness took my thoughts back to a time when it was my turn to be judged. I knew the knives I made and how good they were. What I didn't know was what the judges wanted to see and how they would interpret the message my knives would bring to the show.

Japan To Georgia. Georgia Gov. Zell Miller (left) displays the dangler knife (inset Weyer photo) given him via J. W. Denton (right) and made by Japanese knifemaker Yoshihito Aida as Aida's way of saluting Atlanta for hosting the '96 Summer Olympics.

Happy 40th, Gil! Gil Hibben receives a special knife by Ed Wallace and Rick Hutchings observing Hibben's 40 years as a knifemaker. Making the presentation are Hutchings' and Wallace's children, from right: Stephanie and Christina Wallace and Katie Hutchings.

The Blade Show Mystique

When I walked to my first Blade Show in Knoxville a decade ago, the first bladesmiths I met were Hugh Bartrug and Cleston Sinyard. They greeted me with a smile and a handshake and asked me to join them, our conversation naturally turning to knives and forging steel. I immediately felt welcome. My knives were judged and I found my home in the ABS at the Blade Show.

The challenge to make knives that pass and go beyond the requirements of the ABS test provides the newcomer and the established professional with opportunities limited only by his/her imagination and ability. Success is defined by each individual according to his/her hopes and dreams, for many a success is not measured by the economic aspects of the show, but by the events that will transpire: visits with old friends, shared experiences from the past year and comrades remembered who are absent.

Many of today's makers start their careers with the benefit of hundreds of years of experience. All of this is made possible by the makers of the past, and is passed on to the makers of the future at places like the Blade Show. While some hold on to their private techniques and traditions like a drunk holds on to a fence post for support, others are more than willing to share their discoveries with all who will listen. The gathering of makers, dealers and enthusiasts in the Waverly hotel lobby and hotel rooms to share knife knowledge rapidly advances blade craftsmanship into the 21st century and beyond. The transition advances at a rate that gains momentum with every knife show, with every issue of the periodicals, with every book about knifemaking, and every conversation shared by those who wish to advance the craft for the benefit of all.

Zero Hour

Friday morning came and the 1996 Blade Show began. Greetings between old friends and introductions between those meeting for the first time were heard at breakfast, in the hallways and on the showroom floor. Knife suppliers brought new products for the makers and the makers brought new designs to the show. Displays of Randall knives, old bowies and knives from the American frontier awaited all who wanted to see.

New makers visited the show, asked questions, bought books, videos, materials, knives and equipment in a variety more extensive than any selection I have ever seen at any one place. the Blade Show is so large that it is impossible to take it all in during the time available. An all-encompassing array of how-to seminars were presented on making multiblades, engraving, knife throwing, hammer forging, scrimshaw, flintknappin and many more.

Each year at the Blade magazine Awards Banquet, the Saturday night of the show, a moment of silence is observed for those who remain with us only as memories and by the products of their hand and mind. It was also time to name the winners of the 1996 Blade magazine Knife-Of-The-Year Awards(R), the top factory knives in the industry, as well as the inductees to the Blade magazine Cutlery Hall Of Fame(TM), Blackie Collins and Chuck Buck.

Finally, it had to happen. The 1996 Blade Show came to a close. There was one more evening sharing knife talk in the lobby with a few remaining friends and then we would begin our journey home, our minds filled with new ideas, anxious to get back to work in our shops, where all will prepare for the "family reunion" of the next knife show.

My Old Hat

I still remember the day we met. I walked into the store and there it was hanging on the wire, uncrowned and kind of rough looking I could tell he had had it rough as there was a hole in his side; but, at the same time I knew he was tough and could take it. I asked Cliff, the store manager, what kind of deal he could make and he said twenty-five dollars and he would put on any crown I wanted. The deal was made, and my new hat and partner had the finest "Montana Crease" the Starlight Bar ever saw.

Since that time, we have been through a lot together, and he has never let me down. Age kind of crept up on him and I really didn't notice until I was in the grocery store and noticed this old lady looking at us kinda like I had a sign on me advertising some kind of terrible social disease or something. When I got home, I looked in the only mirror we had in the house. Sure enough, he was looking pretty beat.

I kind of knew time was running out when one day we got caught in a rain and wind storm, and I just wasn't able to cinch him down on my head to where he would stay put; that had never happened before. I feel that the time has come to retire him deep down in my heart, yet I just don't want to do it. Still, it's times like this that you remember the good ones.

There was the time old 67 didn't come into the feed line. She was a cow that I had bought as a heiffer and we never really got along too well. Each year she got tougher to corral for doctoring or calfing. Wet snowflakes were coming down as big as silver dollars and there was nothing to do but start looking for her. My old hat went right out there with me and stuck all the way. He gained about five pounds but kept me dry.

Then there was the day we had to milk out an old cow who had a calf that couldn't get his first meal on his own. She got heated up real quick and was scouring some. It was about 10 below and fresh manure was freezing to her tail. She kept swinging that tail trying to take my head off. All I had to do was turn my head and let him take it full blast. We went to an antique show to pick up some usable horse gear cheap and saw some hat brushes for sale. Instead of being grey, he was mostly green from that old cows tail and needed brushing real bad. I will never forget the look the gal at the antique show gave us when I picked up a hat brush and started cleaning him up. She must a thought the doilies under him were made of gold. We bought the hat brush and told her we didn't need a doilie.

There were many other times. The day the wind blew him into the river and Blue, my black lab, swam out and fetched him back. Funny how your mind works at times like this. Went back to the store and bought another hat for good, planning to retire him, but just couldn't do it. Maybe next year?

Ed Ties The Knot!

Angela bought this knife from Ed when they first met at the 1993 New York Custom Knife Show.

The world of knives and the people who are a part of that world have become my home, my family and source of my greatest pleasure. The best times of my life have always involved blades or people who share the genuine love of knives with an honest desire to know and appreciate them for what they are-the finest functional tools, both as present art form and as a direct link to man's survival throughout history.

All who truly share in the relishing of blades are special friends. Even if I haven't met you in person, the bond is there. There are no strangers in the world of knives. I always knew that if a special lady were to be in my life, she would come from the world of blades so that we could speak the same language, share knife pleasures, and truly come to know and cherish each other.

The Dream Lady

It was at the New York Custom Knife Show at the Roosevelt Hotel in New York City, November 1993, when I met the lady of my dreams, my own personal woman of the world of blades. The show was a busy one. I had shared knife talk with many new friends when I felt the presence of some-

The Rev. Grayson Gowan conducts the ceremony in a field on the Willow Bow Ranch. To Ed's right is his best man, Joe Crofts. At right is the maid of honor, ABS apprentice bladesmith Audra Draper.

Love American Bladesmith Style - a beaming Ed and Angela Fowler after their wedding ceremony.

knew that she was the lady for me. All that I had ever sought in a woman and a partner in life was standing before me. For a time that will always remain in my mind.

She thanked me for my time, placed the knife on my table, then left. I watched as she walked away and wondered if we would ever meet again. I knew that she liked the blade, I knew that she enjoyed our time together, and all I could do was watch her walk away. Then she stopped, talked to one of her friends who was with her, then returned to my table. I was overjoyed!

She renewed our conversation but this time her voice was a little strained. She asked if I would sell her the knife and made me an offer that was a little less than my asking price. I immediately said yes. She paid for it and, in the hope of keeping our contact alive, I handed her a copy of my brochure and video along with the blade. I thanked her and again watched as she walked away. Several times during the show our eyes met and always there was a mutual smile. She returned to the table several times and we exchanged glances, a few words, many thoughts and more.

one very special. I looked toward the show doors and was immediately aware that the lady of my dreams had just entered my life.

Her eyes told me that she was in a world she loved. The excitement she felt radiated from her like the glory of a sunrise. I watched as she walked from table to table, looking knifemakers in the eye, enthusiastically sharing thoughts with those around her, obviously taking in all she saw and heard. From that moment, I was in love!

It seemed like it took her forever to come to my table. Meanwhile, those around me must have thought I had been drinking something other than the mug of orange juice that usually accompanies me to shows. All I could think about was where the woman was and with whom she was talking.

Finally, she came to my table. She looked at my knives and I stood there like a little kid at his first circus. I knew immediately that we were sharing many thoughts. I was afraid that the sound of my heart beating would scare her away. She looked at my blades for some time, then pointed to one and, with a voice I can still hear, asked if it was ok if she picked it up. I told her I would be pleased if she would. The knife she selected had a special curved sheep-horn handle. It was one of those distinct pieces that I can still remember as all the individual tasks came together to complete it.

She looked it over and we talked knives. Actually she asked questions and I tried to answer. I was as close to being tongue tied as I have ever been. She held the blade she had chosen for some time. As our conversation progressed, I

Ed and Angela Fowler on their first date...at what else? A knife show!(Craig S. Feder photo)

"Speaking" By Mail

After the show, I returned to Wyoming and life on the Willow Bow Ranch. Soon, I received a letter from her, complete with her return address. She asked if I remembered her and wrote me a letter filled with a special kind of knife talk. My response was as follows:

"Of course I remember you. How could I forget? From the first time you walked past my table and looked over the knives I had to offer, I remember you. Some times people cross paths and they have been friends all their lives. I remember your hair, your pretty smile, the way you looked at my knives. I remember the way your eyes looked the first time you saw that knife with the curved horn. I was honored that you liked it.

"I remember how you picked it up, looked it over, then left for a while. I wondered why you set it back down on the table. I knew that you liked it. I remember when you came back and made me an offer on the knife. The look in your eyes was the high point of the show for me! I would have sold it to you for whatever price you wanted to pay!

"Sometimes it happens that my knives are chosen by special people and I am deeply honored that they have selected a part of me and taken it into their lives to be a part of them. You are one of those special people to me! Thank you."

My letter went on for several pages. I sent it to her and she answered, and I answered back. As time went on, our letters came more and more frequent. Soon, phone calls added to our getting to know each other. She lived in New York, I lived in Wyoming, 1,978 miles away. I signed up for every knife show in New York in the hopes that we could see each other in person. Time passed and now, thanks to knives, providence, and the help of friends and her family, we are man and wife.

Knife shows bring together the finest people around. The world of blades is a special place, and all the good things in my life come from it. I thank all of you who share knife talk with me and I thank the world of knives for bringing Angela Fowler into my life.

Dick & Dorothy Iiams:
Thanks For The Good Times!

The author (right) and Dick Iiams (pronounced IMES) talk hot steel.

gether the best of times. Often, I became the student and Dick the teacher as we learned together.

Throughout the following years, Dick and Dorothy visited me many times. Each time Dick brought something he'd made or bought to add to my shop. We learned a lot together. When he saw that my knife grips could be improved through a change in methods, he supplied the means that forced me to change my technique and greatly improve my handle designs. He not only supplied me with a lifetime larder of 3-inch-diameter ball bearings, he also was instrumental in developing my freeze-treated forged blades. As we experimented with various steels, his enthusiasm kept each moment, no matter how late the hour, as fresh as a new day.

Together, we not only tested our knives but, as Henry David Thoreau so aptly stated: "Having shingles of thought well dried, we sat and whittled them, trying our knives." Our discussions were of blades, life and events that matter between friends. Dick had a way of keeping life in perspective and his way with humor kept a guy wondering how serious he was.

About eight years ago, as I was heading out to the field to bale hay, a pickup pulled up to my shop. Dick Iiams was driving and his wife, Dorothy, was with him. We'd never met before but Dick's winning ways made us friends from the start. He wanted to learn how to make knives and asked how long I would be baling hay. "Most of the day," I said. As only Dick could, he replied, "Heck, Dorothy can bale the hay; let's make knives!"

At first I was somewhat reluctant to send a lady out to bale hay. I asked her a few questions and she asked me a few in return, leaving no doubt that she knew what she was doing. Within 15 minutes she headed out to the field on my John Deere tractor, my old baler faithfully following behind. Meanwhile, with Dick in tow, I lighted the forge.

Dorothy spent about seven hours baling hay, fixed my aged baler several times when it broke down and, when the hay got too dry to bale, came to the house and started lunch. While Dick and I worked in the shop until dark, she not only fixed dinner but also cleaned my house, which at the time was pretty much a bachelor setup, occupied by my dog, Blue, my cat and me. It was the start of a friendship in which I was honored to participate.

Dick was an extremely able student. His background as an outstanding machinist, attitude toward making knives, and extreme respect for another man's shop made our time to-

Dick Iiams made this stag-handle piece with 52100 blade steel.

Dick Iiams juggling ball bearings. Once a man starts working with ball bearings, it is hard to limit yourself to knives. Dick worked out a juggling act, with what else but 3" diameter ball bearings. It is more work than it looks.

Teamwork

When Dick and I experimented with various damascus steels using ball bearings, each moment was as exciting as a new love. Once we tried to crowd a week's work into two days, mixing combinations of steel for each of us to experiment on individually until our next get-together. We were pushed for time and both near exhaustion. I was forging a primary welding heat on a large billet of steel on my 150-lb. Beaudry hammer when some hot flux fell behind my leather apron and set me afire just below the belt. I couldn't quit or

we would have lost the weld. Without a word, Dick ran into the shop and returned with a water bottle. He poured it down the inside of my smoking apron, extinguishing the fire-too late to save my Levis but just in time to spare my hide. We were so interested in the results of the weld, we didn't even laugh over the event until hours later while splitting up the day's production.

Dick made exceptional high-performance blades and shared both his knowledge and talents with all who asked. He donated knives to a volunteer organization that sponsors what's called "A Hell of a Hunt." It's an annual event that makes the enjoyment of hunting antelope possible for severely handicapped individuals who, without the volunteers' help, couldn't participate.

Dick designed a much-improved platen for my Burr King that not only makes knifemaking much more pleasurable, it also makes slack-belt grinding which renders what I believe to be the optimum convex grind-a precision operation. He also designed and built a belt grinder that would be any knifemaker's instant favorite. His outstanding mechanical abilities, along with a strong desire to apply his talents to the world of knives, have made life better for all who know him.

Our last visit was over dinner in Casper, Wyoming. We spoke of knives, future experiments and times past. Two weeks later a cat scan revealed a cyst on his brain. Within hours he was in surgery and dropped into a coma from which he has yet to return.

I have one of his knives and some equipment that he made for me, as well as many fond memories of good times. Once again I hear the message: The past is over; our future remains unknown. All we have for certain is this single, precious moment. The art of living well is to breathe in each and every moment and enjoy to the fullest the nectar it has to offer. Each moment with a loved one, friend or nature, or time spent visiting a craftsman through his art, is our most precious gift. If you own an Iiams knife, you have the blade of a man I believe to be one of the finest knifemakers of all time.

To Dick Iiams, knifemaker, friend and outstanding citizen of the world of blades, and to Dorothy, who not only fully supported his commitment to making a better knife but who continues to stand by his side with all the love and devotion any man could ask for: Thanks for the good times.

Thanks, Pilgrims

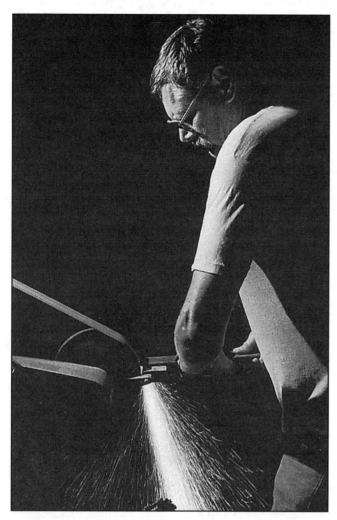

The author thanks suppliers for the broad selection of grinders (here's maker Chuck Stapel busy at the wheel), buffer and etching solutions they provide.

This Thanksgiving, I want to thank all of you who take the time to read my stories. Many of you write or call me personally commenting on various issues, and I find these contacts rewarding. I also enjoy talking to you when you stop and visit at knife shows.

I'm not only thankful for the shared thoughts when you like what I write, I also thank those who take issue with some of my articles. When blades are openly discussed, everyone gains. Many aspects of cutlery philosophy, design and construction are controversial, and I embrace the opportunity to explore all new and old territories in the world of knives.

Thanks and welcome to the new cutlers. I'm proud of the quality of today's blades. Knifemakers are getting better all the time. The quality of contemporary blades is due to the

many makers who constantly improve their skills to provide the enthusiast with knives to fit his/her desires.

Thanks to the suppliers, who also contribute to the quality and diversity of modern knives. There was a time when the maker profiled blades with files and stones. Now, abrasives are better than ever. There's a broad selection of grinders, buffers and etching solutions. There are waxes to keep blades from rusting, polishes to make them shine and cases in which to keep them. There is also a great selection of materials from which to choose - steels, ceramics, titanium and other metals - as well as custom heat treaters to push the blade to its limit. The variety of grip materials makes possible an unlimited number of unique handle designs, making the place where the hand and the knife meet all the better.

The suppliers also do a lot of educating when new and established makers come to them to talk blades. They know what the new materials do and how to work them, and are constantly bringing new technology to the world of knives.

The photographers who keep you informed by telling it all in one picture make cutlery magazines more enjoyable and give you a taste of knives you may never experience in person. The quality of their photos and innovative backgrounds

Thanks to the children who take an interest in contributing, either by doing extra chores or making blades, such as this copper one by Christopher Scott.

speak of their devotion to making looking at knives more entertaining and informative.

Thanks to Krause Publications and Dave Kowalski for investing in the "Blade" magazine and making "Blade" available to more potential readers than ever before. Krause, its enthusiastic and knowledgeable staff and the technology it brings to the table, injects new life and vitality into the world of knives. This past year, *Fighting Knives* ceased publication. The loss of any member of the cutlery industry is disturbing. Competition keeps everyone sharp, criticism keeps everybody on the right track, and *Fighting Knives* didn't pull any punches.

A special thanks goes to all who support blade interests. To all the families, from the cat who keeps the shop free of mice, to the wives who work to keep makers in the shop (especially for that cup of coffee at two in the morning, and for all they do that gives their spouses the time and means for making the world of knives a nice place to be). Thanks to the children who take an interest in contributing, either by making blades or doing extra chores. Without their sharing time and unselfish support, the cutlery industry would lack the bounty it now has.

Thanks to all who have welcomed and encouraged new explorers to the world of knives, from the collectors and enthusiasts who share their knowledge with the new guy, to the makers who teach the beginner, to the mothers and grandmothers who proclaimed their joy when receiving that first blade as a gift, and even used it as best they could when the budding maker was around.

Thanks to the successful pioneers who have confidently shared their discoveries, expanding the frontiers and allowing the knifemaking art to rapidly advance to levels beyond the boundaries of tradition.

The harvest of the world of knives is as diverse as all those who enjoy their visits to it. The larder is full, each contributor having found his/her own cherished fruit. From the stone-age blade, to the most complex and elegant design, from the rusted pocketknife to the most complex metallurgical text, there is something for everyone. Best of all are the good times shared. Thank you one and all.

CHAPTER 3

Forging
&
Heat Treating

The following concepts were written as a result of our search for a better knife. The experiments that lead to these articles ate up a lot of steel, propane and time. For each success there were many failures. When I received my ABS Journeyman Stamp, I thought I knew it all! Now, today, after a lifetime working with knives, I have more questions than answers. Some of these articles proved very controversial; some were hardly noticed. I was never able to predict which would encourage what response. They were not written to attack any individual or group; rather, the intention was to promote the development of better knives.

The more who join in the search for the Excalibur of tomorrow, the better future knives will be, and the experience will offer nourishment for all. Each individual has a contribution to make, be it an improved zipper for a knife case, or a new steel. One may look at a knife through their unique eye, ask a new question or answer what no one has ever been able to answer. Be it a poem or a knife, you can make a difference.

Relive The Past With Bronzed Blades

Early in August 1977, I was cleaning my shop one evening. Laying behind the grinder was a wire Damascus blade that I had forged, hardened and etched, then discarded due to some flaws that I felt were too serious to allow a serviceable blade. The faults took the form of black pits in the dark-etched blade.

I took the blade to the welding table and tried to flow brass into the pits. I fluxed then melted brass onto the blade. Rather than the brass merely flowing into the pits, it covered the entire blade. I then ground the excess brass off, polished, hardened, tempered, then etched the blade in ferric chloride. The results were better than expected. Most of the faults that had been so prominent had disappeared. Brass had flowed into places where there had been no visible faults previously. Some of the dark pits had filled with brass and the desired effect was realized. The brass contrasted nicely with the greys and blacks of the etched wire Damascus blade.

I tried using the blade on some pine and found that the edge chipped badly. Normally the only tempering required to make one of my wire Damascus blades tough enough to prevent the edge from chipping is a triple 385° F-draw. I tempered the blade three times at 400° but it still chipped out. I tried another triple draw at 415° and the blade quit chipping and cut very well. I tested the blade on hemp rope and was extremely pleased with the cutting ability of the blade. Remember, this was a blade that I had discarded due to imperfect welds.

Since then, I have bronzed a number of my wire Damascus blades and found them to be rather fascinating. For example, all bronzed blades do not require the higher drawing temperature; most do, but not all. Some edges quit chipping at 385° draw, some at 400°, some at 415° and some at 425°.

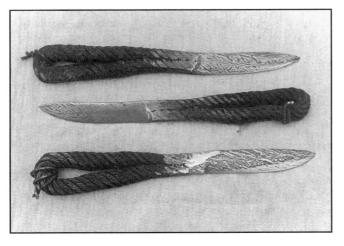

The three blades after the completion of Ed's testing. Note that the bronzed blade (bottom) did not lose as much steel as the other two. (Fowler photo)

To test the functional aspects of the bronzed blade, I cut three 14 inch lengths from a single piece of 5/16-inch steel cable. The three lengths were all forged into blades on the same day. Forging was simple. I merely doubled the cable and forge welded the ends together, the loop forming the knife handle.

Blade one was prepared the same way as one of my standard knives. Blades two and three were heated, fluxed, not bronzed and bronzed, respectively. These blades were then placed in a bucket of vermiculite to cool from the cherry-red heat. All three were then sanded to similar blade shapes and hardened using Brownell's Tough Quench. All three were tempered three times at 385°. I sharpened the blades and found all three to be adequately tempered. The bronzed blade did not require the expected higher temperature for tempering.

The completed knives were tested by alternately cutting repeatedly on a single length of 3/4 inch hemp rope. The knives were resharpened after each test. I terminated each test when the edge lost what I call its ability to aggressively cut. I could have forced the blade to cut more times, but in the interest of preventing necessary fatigue and wasting expensive rope, I quit when I could feel a loss in cutting efficiency. Following are the results of the cutting tests:

Cuts in each test						Total
Test	1	2	3	4	5	cuts
1) Standard wire Damascus	14	15	8	5	12	54
2) Flame-treated wire Damascus	7	4	3	3	3	20
3) Bronzed-wire Damascus	15	13	4	11	14	57

As the table shows, the standard blade and the bronzed blade cut very well. One section of the rope was much tougher to cut than the rest of the rope, which accounts for the third and fourth series of cuts with knives one and three. I was surprised by the performance of knife No. 2 (the fluxed and flame-treated blade, no brass). For some reason this blade did not want to cut. Some day I will undertake another series of trials to find out why.

Two more blades were then forged from a billet of wire Damascus that consisted of 10, 14-inch pieces of wire rope. One of the blades was bronzed, then both were hardened in an oil bath of Brownell's Tough Quench. Both were then triple drawn in an oven at 385°. The unbronzed blade did not chip out when tested, but the bronzed blade did. The bronzed blade was then triple drawn at 415°. After the higher draw it quit chipping and the test proceeded. Here are the results:

Cuts in each test

Test	1	2	3	4	5	
Bronzed blade	17	14	16	16	50	113
Unbronzed blade	12	14	18	14	49	107

(In test 5, I ran out of rope and switched to another rope smaller in diameter. This accounts for the larger number of cuts.)

The test results indicate that as far as cutting ability, the bronzed blade is as good as the unbronzed blade, maybe just a little better. The requirement of a higher draw temperature seems to indicate that some alloying of metal occurs when blades are bronzed. The bronzed blades are softer than the unbronzed blades when properly tempered. This does not have a negative effect upon the blade's ability to cut the material in these tests. As for the appearance of bronzed blades, the brass is not always visible to the naked eye. A perfectly welded blade will have little brass showing. I feel that copper flows into the blade during the etching process in the form of a blue-green precipitate.

There is a special significance to my experiments. Every knife enthusiast has read or heard about the legendary bronzed blades of ancient times that had superior cutting abilities. Previous to the coming of the Iron Age, copper, silver and gold were the metals of the day. Bronze was possibly the "in" metal for cutting tools at one time. Then came the Iron Age and new blade materials came on the scene.

As man was experimenting with the new materials of the Iron Age, his knowledge was in is infancy. The bronze blades of the then recent past were in all probability not vastly inferior to the "new" iron blades, for a time at least. For the old knifemaker who was learning to use the metals of the Iron Age, it very well could have been a logical step for him to try to mix the old with the new. Considering that knowledge about the "new" materials was rather scanty, there had to have been some blends of the past with the present.

The first time I bronzed an inferior blade, it became an extremely serviceable blade. Imagine the old knifemaker looking over his first knife of the Iron Age, seeing the imper-

The bronzed blade slightly outcuts the unbronzed blades in the author's cutting.

fections in the new blade and adding some of the bronze from the scrap pile to enhance his new blade's cutting ability. He would have had a ready market for his product. Just as when you put on a new hat or pair of shoes without reminiscing about the comfort of the old ones, so would have ancient man remembered the advantages of bronzed blades when he acquired his first iron blade. I feel that in all probability the market was there for a bronzed blade.

Every now and then an historian makes a statement about legendary bronze blades that hardened when heated to a cherry-red and quenched in water. We all know that brass or bronze becomes softer when treated in such a manner. But a bronzed steel blade becomes harder when heated and quenched.

Suppose the bronze blades that historians refer to were, in actuality, bronzed-steel blades? I feel that the bronzed-steel blade could have and, in all probability, did exist and deserves a place in history. Possibly some of the readers of this article would have more knowledge in this area and would like to share their thoughts on the issue. I, for one, would like to read them.

The Tell-Tale Etch:
How To Unlock The True Nature Of The Steel

Etched with ferric chloride, the grain structure in the 52100 steel is obvious. The edge is hard and doesn't etch as dark as the soft back of the blade. Note the three separate quenches on the ricasso. Also visible are small light dots throughout the blade. While the dots are not always present in blades that have been treated with a superlative thermal treatment, they do show up every now and then just to make me smile.

When you judge a knife solely on its cosmetic features, you are much like the man buying used car. Having to rely on what he can see and hear, he looks over the paint job, listens to the motor and kicks the tires in an attempt to predict the performance of his next major purchase. Much like the used car, the essence of the blade remains hidden under the polish. The blade may or may not be the high-performance cutting instrument you can depend on when the chips are down. Grind lines, symmetry and fit and finish are all clues to the abilities of the maker, but there is a lot more to a high-performance blade than these attributes alone can predict.

The best way to evaluate a knife is to buy it, take it home, cut with it, sharpen it, cut with it again and compare it to the cutting ability of another blade. Then put the blade in a vise, flex it to a 90-degree angle, then break it and examine the crystalline structure of the steel. You now have a good indicator of the performance ability of the blade-trouble is, the knife doesn't work anymore.

The true nature of any piece of steel can be revealed in a laboratory but a lab test is expensive and may destroy the knife's usefulness. Knowing the nature of the blade steel is one essential consideration when evaluating a knife's potential. Some steels produce knife blades that are superior to others. Additional attributes that contribute are the mechanical and thermal treatments used to develop the hardness and grain structure of the finished blade.

Wouldn't it be nice if there were a crystal ball that provided insight into the true nature of the steel, a crystal ball that

could open significant aspects of the history of the steel for your inspection? We need a crystal ball that, much like Edgar Allan Poe's "Tell Tale Heart," can reveal the secrets hidden behind the veil of polish, providing insight into the secrets of the knife and maker.

One such crystal ball is available to the serious student of knives. It's called the etched blade. Etching a polished blade can unveil the secrets heretofore known only to those who made the blade. The information provided by etching can reveal aspects of the blade that otherwise may go unnoticed by the maker. Etching provides another means of quality control to the maker by helping him fine tune his abilities.

I recommend that all blades used in the field should be etched. Etching can provide an honest statement about the true nature of the steel in a blade. This doesn't mean that etching is infallible; there is a way around any fence. Etching a blade is simply one way to increase the probability that an honest statement is being made concerning the knife. Patterns in the steel revealed by etching are significant indicators of the thermal and mechanical treatments used to create the final nature of the blade as a cutting instrument.

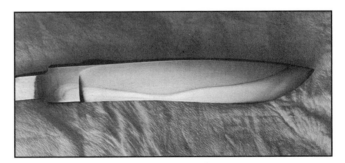

The temper line in this blade clearly expresses the fact that this blade was __NOT__ properly hardened. The sofr portion of the blade dips nearly to the edge.

Etching is usually accomplished by submerging the blade in a diluted acid solution or ferric chloride (also known as Archer Etchant, available at Radio Shack stores). I prefer ferric chloride because it is relatively safe and readily available. (Warning: Observe cautions written on the label.) Etching a blade in ferric chloride is normally done as follows:

Dilute the etchant solution with water, one part ferric chloride to four parts water. Polish the blade and wipe it clean, then submerge the blade in the etchant. Allow the etchant to work on the steel for five to 10 minutes. Remove the blade and submerge it in a strong solution of tri-sodium phosphate (or TSP, available at most hardware stores) to stop the action of the ferric chloride. Soak the blade in the TSP for several minutes, then wash it in water. The blade can be buffed or hand rubbed with fine (1,200-grit) sandpaper to reveal the grain structure. If you need to etch the blade longer, repeat the process until the desired degree of etching is reached.

I am not suggesting that you etch all of the knives that you own. Etching is the task of the knifemaker who has the knowledge and equipment to do the job right. Etching is a fairly simple task and can answer a lot of questions that are usually asked when a blade is evaluated. A light etch can reveal a temper line in a polished blade. The temper line is one of the distinctive features of a top-notch blade. A deeper etch can reveal the pattern in a crystalline or mechanical Damascus blade.

Knives are made and purchased for many reasons. A knife may be made to be pleasing to the, eye. It is OK to make and sell a knife for whatever reason on which two people can agree. This discussion is designed to increase the understanding of the etched blade.

The informed individual can read an etched blade like a book. Future articles will explore the "telltale heart" of the etched blade to a greater degree. I don't profess to know it all; the more we discuss the etched blade, the greater our understanding. At one time I considered it almost sacrilegious to etch any blade other than a mechanical Damascus blade. Then I started experimenting with new steels and learned how informative etching a blade could be. Etching all of my blades has made me a better knifemaker and continues to help improve my skills.

I know that there are a lot of knives that are high-performance examples of the knifemaker's art. The etched blade, however, has a way of putting all the cards face up on the table. In the game of life I kind of like it that way-you know where you stand. I feel more confident carrying an etched blade simply because I know more about it. Etching doesn't offer a 100 percent guarantee. But the etched blade provides the man using it with fewer surprises, when the chips are down, than its polished cousin.

How to Heat Treat: The Spirit Of The Forged Blade

Many variables determine the quality of the forged blade. Most of them can only be hypothetically considered by the bladesmith in his privately financed shop hundreds of miles from a sophisticated laboratory. Some hypothetical constructs have become rather obvious and have repeated themselves with sufficient reliability in my experience, so I am willing to stick my neck out and claim a strong degree of validity in their occurrence.

For example: The relationship of the degree of forging to blade performance. Forge a blade out of 1/8-by-1-by-6-inch stock and compare it to a blade forged from 3/8-by-2-by-4-inch stock; the blade forged from the larger stock will out-cut the minimally forged blade every time. This is especially true of 5160 steel, and to a lesser but still significant degree, with bearing-quality 52100 steel. The larger the dimensions of the original steel billet (and therefore the greater the degree of forging required to produce a knife), the better the blade will perform.

High-performance blades are the result of knowledgeable forging and sophisticated thermal treatments. Performance in this case is defined as the blade's ability to cut and to be tough, strong and easy to sharpen. Consider the terms individually. The ability to cut is self-explanatory: The blade must aggressively cut the material it is designed to cut.

A blade is tough when it can be flexed to 90 ° without breaking and the cutting edge can be flexed without chipping under normal use.

Strength means resistance to bending. A strong blade flexes over its entire length rather than looking like a creased piece of paper after being flexed to 90°. High performance blades do not just happen; they are the result of planning. To get the best out of a steel, read all the information concerning it. Manufacturers are one source of information. All you need do is ask. Old and new metallurgical books are also great sources. Read with an open mind and apply what you read without prejudice.

The following discussion on forging and heat treating deals specifically with two steels: 5160 and bearing-quality 52100. The techniques discussed may or may not apply to other steels but have worked for me and have been developed over a period of years involving a lot of experiments and discussion with other knifemakers. The reader who applies these concepts to other steels may have to vary from the methods and materials discussed.

Forging

The greater the amount of proper forging at the correct temperature to form a blade, the greater the potential quality of the finished blade. Forging can significantly increase the effectiveness of future thermal treatments. The greatest harm a bladesmith can do while forging is to overheat the steel. A blade that has been overheated can look fine when finished, but its performance will be significantly reduced. Overheating creates coarse grain and burns out carbon. Forge steel while it is too cold and it can crack or break, and all you have is scrap.

Normalizing

There was a time when I didn't believe that normalizing was necessary. I am now a believer. Forged blades normalized prior to annealing may or may not cut better than blades that were only annealed, but they tend to warp less significantly. Normalizing is a stress-relieving operation necessary for all forged blades.

After the last forging heat, uniformly heat the blade (I heat the blade in my forge) to slightly above critical temperature. Critical temperature is the temperature that 52100 and 5160 cease to be magnetic. When the blade has been heated to the point where it is no longer attracted to the magnet, allow the blade to cool to room temperature in air. I use a homemade aluminum rack to hold the blade while it cools.

Annealing

Once the blade has been normalized, uniformly heat the blade to the low end of the critical temperature. Use great care to avoid overheating. When the blade is no longer attracted to the magnet, it is hot enough. Submerge the blade into a bucket of vermiculite (available through most insulation suppliers) and allow it to cool slowly to room temperature. Proper annealing ensures a fine grain structure in the steel prior to hardening the blade. Annealing differs from normalizing in that annealing requires a much slower cooling rate.

Preparing The Annealed Blade For Hardening

Forge all of your blades slightly oversize. After normalizing and annealing, grind the blade to its approximate final shape, leaving it 3-1/32 to 1/8 inch oversize in the area that surrounds what will be the cutting edge. An oversized hardened blade will require more time and materials to grind to final shape than grinding an annealed blade to final shape.

This extra effort is well worth it. The extra steel envelops and protects the part of the blade that will become the cutting edge from the negative effects of the hardening process, specifically from the loss of carbon. This greatly increases the probability of a high-performance forged knife blade. Before I realized this, my forged blades did not reach peak performance until they had been sharpened several times, which removed the steel that had lost carbon during the hardening process.

Grinding Prior To Hardening

Use a 36-grit belt to get the desired shape (3/32- to 1/8-

inch oversize in the edge area). Polish out all scratches with 60-, 180-, then 500-grit belts. Removing all scratches is necessary, as any scratches around the area of the blade to be hardened can result in weak spots or cracks that can occur when the blade is subjected to the stress of hardening.

Quenching Oil

Use Texaco Type A quenching oil or an equivalent to harden 5160 and 52100. This oil is a "slow" quenching oil that I am told is essentially mineral oil. My quench tank was homemade by splitting a 4-1/2-inch in diameter heavy duty pipe about 18 inches long, and welding a couple of ends and legs onto it. The tank holds enough quenching oil to effectively handle the heat load from bird and trout blades to larger camp knives.

In the tank I place a homemade aluminum table that is adjustable for depth. This provides an adjustable platform to place the heated blade on in the oil, thus ensuring precision control of the depth of the blade in the oil. I drilled as many 3/8-inch holes in the table as possible. The holes guarantee maximum circulation of the oil around the heated blade during quenching.

Due to the viscosity of the quenching oil, you must preheat the oil before quenching. The cooler the oil, the slower it cools the blade. Warm the oil and it circulates better and cools quicker. When hardening 5160 and bearing-quality 52100 steels, pre-heat the oil to 160° F. Use a thermometer to measure the oil temperature. Any thermometer ranging from 70-200° F should do. A poultry thermometer works fine.

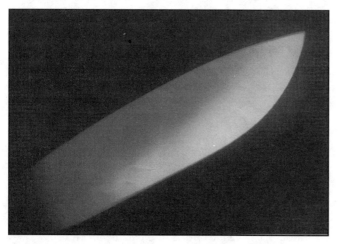

The color pattern you want to see in the blade just before quenching in oil. The back of the blade is not hot enough to completely harden. Only the edge portion is non-magnetic.

Heating The Blade Prior To Hardening

Heating the blade prior to a hardening heat treating is the spirit of the forged blade. Properly performed and the blade soars with the eagles; improperly done and the blade may be

no better than the poorest stock removal one. Many blades become poor performers due to poor heating methods. Overheat the blade and you lose all of the qualities that you have worked for up to this point; specifically, carbon and fine grain structure.

At this point, heat your blade with an oxyacetylene torch equipped with a Victor #3 tip. Turn the oxygen and acetylene pressure down to the point that the flame is "quiet," using much less pressure than for welding with the #3 tip. To reduce carbon loss and to keep the flame as "soft" as possible, use a 2x flame (identified by an acetylene feather twice as long as the inner cone). Run just enough pressure to avoid flashback and backfire.

HEAT THE BLADE SLOWLY, starting at the ricasso and working slowly and uniformly over the entire lower third of the blade. To **AVOID HOT SPOTS**, keep the flame moving constantly along the blade. If necessary, practice this step on a piece of scrap until you can 'paint' the color into the blade with the dexterity of a master. This is probably the most difficult skill to learn. You have to work at it. Only you will know when this step is performed improperly. This is one aspect of bladesmithing where the knifemaker's ethics are of the utmost importance. It is easy to polish up and sell a blade that is of poor quality, so this is one aspect of quality that is between you and your conscience.

Continuously check your blade's temperature with a magnet. As soon as the lower third of the blade is non-magnetic, **QUENCH IMMEDIATELY**. There is no benefit and a lot to lose by holding the blade at critical temperature for more than several seconds when hardening 5160 and 52100.

NEVER HEAT THE TANG prior to quenching; it needs to be tough, not hard. **HEAT SLOWLY, HEAT UNIFORMLY, QUENCH PROMPTLY.** Submerge the tip of the blade into the oil first, hold for several seconds, then "rock" the rest of the cutting edge into the oil. The homemade quench table controls the depth of the quench. Hold for about seven seconds, then raise the back of the blade thus submerging the tip for a couple of seconds. Then rock back down again to submerge the rest of the cutting edge. Repeat this procedure until the color is completely out of the blade, then submerge the entire blade in the oil below the table and let the blade cool to room temperature in the oil. This slows cooling and makes for a better blade. 5160 blades subjected to extensive forging respond extremely well to multiple quenching.

Once the blade cools to room temperature in the oil, remove the blade from the oil and test for hardness with a file. The file will slide across the blade if the blade has hardened. If the file bites into the blade, the blade has not hardened and you must reheat and quench.

If the blade hardened, sand out the file scratches and repeat the quenching (hardening) operation and test again. Repeat the procedure a third time, letting the blade cool in oil each time to room temperature. You will find that the blade seems softer when tested with the file after each successive quench. This is due to a progressive refinement of the grain structure. These blades will sharpen easier and cut longer than single-quenched 5160 and 52100 blades. Usually my 5160 multiple-quench blades so treated will flex to 90° without a soft-back draw or tempering.

However, temper all 5160 blades for three two-hour draws in an oven at 350° F, allowing the blade to air cool to room temperature between each tempering. I strongly recommend this final thermal treatment. Temperatures required for proper tempering may vary with the steel used.

Hardening Bearing-Quality 52100 Steel

Hardening bearing-quality 52100 steel requires a slightly different hardening procedure. After hardening the blade and allowing it to cool in the oil to room temperature, keep the blade at room temperature at least 24 hours between each quenching cycle. Blades hardened at 24-hour intervals cut better, and demonstrate greater strength and toughness than 52100 blades hardened three times in one day.

My first high-performance forged 52100 blade received 24-hour intervals between quenches by accident. I worked for months to re-discover this event. This points out the necessity of keeping accurate notes when experimenting. I would have saved a great deal of time and frustration had I recorded all information rather than just what I felt was important at the time.

Tempering Bearing-Quality 52100 Steel Blades

Temper bearing-quality 52100 steel blades three times at 375° F, allowing them to air cool to room temperature between heats. Grind the blade to final shape, taking off the excess steel purposefully left around the edge. Once the blade is sharpened, test edge toughness by flexing it over a brass rod (see Wayne Goddard's article on knife testing in December 1990 Blade). Should a blade chip in this test, temper the blade as before, increasing the draw (tempering) temperature by 25° F, then resharpen the edge and test again.

Once the cutting edge passes the flex test, re-sharpen the edge and grind off the part that has been flexed, as this steel will have been weakened from the flexing. Once the edge has been resharpened, proceed with the cutting tests. There is no benefit in testing a blade's cutting ability before the flex test. An edge that chips out is not a blade on which you can depend.

Bearing-quality 52100 steel blades are tough and normally pass the 90° flex test without cracking or breaking. Their strength is evidenced by the force required to flex them,

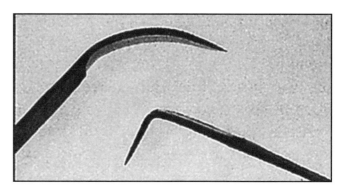

Both test blades were flexed to 90°, the top one multiple edge quenched and triple drawn at 375°F. The bearing-quality 52100 steel was exceptionally strong requiring considerable force to flex it the 90°. The blade didn't crack or break. The blade flexed over the entire length between the ricasso and the tip held in the vise. The blade then partially returned to straight. The lower blade didn't break but it was easy to bend and remained bent. It folded like a piece of paper. All flex was in one area only. It didn't even try to return to straight. (Fowler photo)

and also by the fact that they flex along the entire length of the blade, much like the limb of a long bow. These blades are also easy to sharpen, matching up perfectly with the Norton India oil stone to dress a dulled blade back to shaving condition in seconds. Best of all, they cut better than any all around performance blade. The only blades that out-cut them broke like a piece of glass when subjected to the 90° flex test.

Summary

Multiple quenching produces an ultra-fine grain structure when performed on 5160 and 52100 steels, providing the blades have been properly forged. This ultra-fine grain structure significantly contributes to increased blade performance. There is a lot more to a high performance forged blade than can be covered in a single article. I have tried to cover topics that seem to be the greatest contributors to the confusion surrounding the forged blade.

The forged blade is the key to high performance blades of the future. Multiple quenching is one of the trade secrets of high-performance blades of the past. I hope this article will encourage other bladesmiths to experiment and report their results. As long as the lines of communication are kept open, the forged blade will continue to provide the man who loves to make or use knives a source of satisfaction and enjoyment.

The Process Of Multiple Quench

When I first started making knives, it was widely believed that when hardening a blade, should the blade not harden on the first quench, it was necessary to start from scratch, and anneal the blade to its state before the failed hardening, then harden it again. To my knowledge no one had explored the performance of blades that had been hardened more than once. Most knifemakers, including myself, considered subjecting blades to multiple hardening cycles pure folly and probably detrimental to the qualities of the blade.

At first I could not believe the superior qualities indicated by the testing of multiple quench blades. Test blade after test blade told me the same thing, 'SUCCESS.' As I came to believe in the process, I talked to other knifemakers, most thought I was nuts. Wayne Goddard took me seriously, and agreed to participate in experiments related in the article. Wayne encouraged me to write the article and assisted in the numerous revisions necessary to get it ready to submit for publication.

Today many knifemakers who seek high-performance blades use the multiple quench principle regularly. I have never seen or heard of a multiple quench forged blade failing performance tests such as the well known ABS tests, as long as certain guidelines are followed. 5160 steel, Texaco Type A quenching fluid (or equivalent grade heat treating oil) and dedication to learning how to do it right is all it takes. Many try to substitute the quenching oil, some are successful, but most of the failures are knives that were quenched in something other than Texaco Type A or an equivalent oil

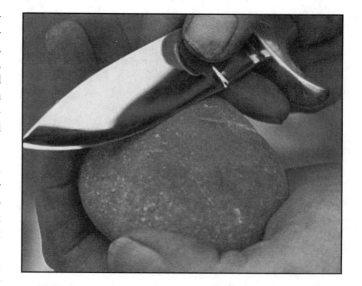

Incidentally, this article became one of the most expensive articles I ever wrote. I received as many questions and comments concerning the techniques from knifemakers, but the response from readers wanting to obtain a "genuine Wyoming Sharpening Stone" like the one in the photo was overwhelming. The picture, with it's quotation, was meant to imply that the knives could be sharpened on a stone that was just a regular rock picked up off of the ground. I spent more on postage and phone calls explaining than I got paid for the article.

Multiple Quenching

by Ed Fowler & Wayne Goddard

Sometimes things come together in a strange way. I (Ed) stumbled onto the value of multiple quenching following what I considered to be a series of errors. The following evening I called Wayne to discuss the results of my initial experiment. Wayne is the man who taught me how to make wire Damascus blades and through the years, the two of us have corresponded about knives and knifemaking at great lengths. Anytime I stumble upon something interesting, Wayne is the man that I contact. His vast knowledge coupled with his empirical sense of order has proven to be invaluable throughout the years.

Ed Fowler is caught at work in the "grinding department."

We had been planning to spend a week in my shop following the Blade Show one-year. We decided that the week in my shop would be devoted to designing and conducting a series of tests that would determine the value of multiple quench blades. Wayne stated that he had read about multiple quenches in an old metallurgy book, and while at the Blade

Show in Tennessee, Al Pendray produced an old handbook that recommends multiple quenches for some steels. Had I not already witnessed what appeared to be superior cutting performance by multiple quenched blades, I would not have believed how significantly the cutting ability of a blade could be enhanced.

While at the show, we discussed the possibility of designing an experiment that would compare the cutting ability of multiple quenched blades to that of single quenched blades. We decided that we would also include stock removal blades of the same steel, subjecting them to the same variations in hardening techniques, and thus answering for ourselves whether or not forging would actually enhance a blades ability to cut.

The blades were made and all initial testing was done in Ed Fowler's shop near Riverton, Wyoming, starting on May 23 and finishing on May 30, 1990. We selected a new bar of 5160 steel that was more than long enough to supply the steel for four blades. The first seven inches of bar was split in two, and two stock removal blades were ground from these pieces. Then two blades were forged from the original bar. Please note that the bar was 1-3/4 inches wide and 3/8-inch thick. This required quite a bit of forging to reduce the bar to the size of the blades that were used in this experiment. The blades size ended up being 3/16 x 3/4 x 4-1/8 inches.

All four blades were then ground to the same dimensions. In order to eliminate as many variable as possible, the tangs of all four knives were also similar and drilled in order that the same handle could be bolted to them individually for the cutting tests.

Hardening

All four blades were quenched in Texaco Type A quenching oil. As there was no requirement in this for a soft back blade, and in order to eliminate as many unnecessary variables as possible, the entire blade of each knife was hardened.

One stock removal blade and one forged blade were randomly selected from the four blades, and they were heated and quenched in the usual manner. The Texaco Type A quenching oil was preheated to 120° F. and maintained between 120-150 ° F. Then the two remaining blades, one stock removal and one forged, were heated, quenched, allowed to air cool and then quenched a second and third time, being allowed to air cool before heating again. All scale was removed between heats.

The first perceptible difference in the blades was noted at this time as the stock removal blades had a much tougher scale on them after hardening than the forged blades. The forged blades could be easily cleaned up while the stock removal blades required a little extra elbow grease. All four blades were then placed in an oven, preheated to 320° F. for 30 minutes, allowed to air cool, and then placed back in the oven for a total of three 30 minutes soaks at 320° F.

Sharpening

The blades were then individually sharpened, using what is termed the "Moran Edge". We took turns sharpening between tests.

Testing

All cutting tests were performed cutting a single strand from a 1-inch diameter hemp rope. The rope was clean and new. Each blade was individually bolted into the same handle by the one of us who was not doing the cutting. The man doing the cutting did not know which blade he was testing. Each blade was tested on the rope; cutting until it lost the ability to aggressively cut the rope. When the man who was cutting felt that this point was reached, the knife was handed to the other man who tried a few cuts to verify that the blade had lost its ability to aggressively cut, and then the number of cuts was recorded.

The results speak for themselves. It is pretty hard to sharpen knives exactly the same time after time. We both spent a lot of time discussing and experimenting with our sharpening techniques.

The forged triple quenched blade easily and consistently out-performed the other knives in this test. It cut 3.14 times better than the stock removal single quench blade.

$$\frac{\textit{forged triple quenched blade - 509 cuts}}{\textit{stock removal single quenched - 162 cuts}} = 3.14$$

2.6 times better than the stock removal triple quenched blade-

$$\frac{\textit{forged triple quenched blade - 509 cuts}}{\textit{stock removal single quenched - 195 cuts}} = 2.6$$

and 1.9 times better than the forged single quench blade-

$$\frac{\textit{forged triple quenched blade - 509 cuts}}{\textit{stock removal single quenched - 269 cuts}} = 1.9$$

The cutting order of the knives was randomly determined. The man cutting did not know which blade he was cutting with, and therefore, the probability for error should be quite low. We definitely feel that this was a fairly designed test, comparing not only the forged blade against the stock removal blade, but also the value of multiple quenches versus single quenches as it pertains to turning out a blade capable of superior performance.

As noted earlier, the forged blades were forged from rather large pieces of steel, thus requiring quite a bit of forging. We feel that the more a piece of steel is reduced in cross section by forging at the proper temperature, the greater the probability of turning out a superior knife blade.

Compare the difference between the two stock removal blades. The triple quenched stock removal blade out-cuts the single quenched stock removal blade by 1.2 times. Now compare the forged triple quenched blade over the forged single quenched blade. 509 cuts versus 296 cuts spells a 1.9 difference. It becomes fairly obvious that the forging greatly enhances the beneficial effects of the multiple quench.

Legend makes great claims for certain knifemakers of yesterday. Knives still available for testing indicate that some knives were superior. When the secrets of success die with the discoverer, we all lose progress and must wait for the events that came together for the first success to repeat themselves again. Many times the information was there to be shared and either no one listened, or, if they heard it, they didn't believe or couldn't use the information to any advantage.

Through the unselfish sharing of information, we have the ability to advance the art of knifemaking to levels never possible without it. The blacksmith of yesterday and the knifemaker of today work independently without the benefit of unlimited technical assistance. Each is on his own in his privately financed shop. Through the sharing of information, we can utilize the experience of thousands of individuals, each contributing to benefit the art of knife making.

After we accidentally discovered the benefits of the multiple quench, Wayne advised me that Al Pendray was using a multiple quench on his blades. When Wayne mentioned this, I vaguely remembered reading an article to that effect about Al's knives. The trouble was, I read it and didn't integrate it to the extent that I tried it. Hopefully, the information in this article will convince more knifemakers to try multiple quenches and report their results.

In summary, I'd like to mention that Wayne and I did a lot more experimenting than is reported upon here. The key conclusion we came to relative to the multiple quench process is forging enhances the effect of the multiple quench. I have worked with 0-1, 440c, 52100, wire and layer Damascus and in every case the results have been spectacular. I feel that the reason these blades cut so well is because we've achieved an extremely fine crystal in the edge as well as possibly "grain flow".

The trouble with experimenting is that it takes a lot of time, and you don't get paid for the failures. You can get so enthusiastic about the experiment, that everything else is forgotten. When you hit upon something that really works, like the multiple quench, it is all worth it

Multiple Quench cutting tests

Knife #	Type	Quench #	Test Cuts	Total
#1	Stock Removal	Single	44..35..37..47	163*
#2	Stock Removal	Triple	49..44..45..57	195*
#3	Forged	Single	78..77..60..54	269*
#4	Forged	Triple	120..127..132..130	509*

•Average cuts per knife in the same sequence as above: 40, 48, 67, and 127.

The authors would like to remind readers that this experiment utilized 5160 steel. Other steels may or may not respond to multiple quenching techniques. Variations in quenching medium may be required for other steels, and techniques may have to be varied, too. Only extensive testing will reveal if this method will work with other steels.

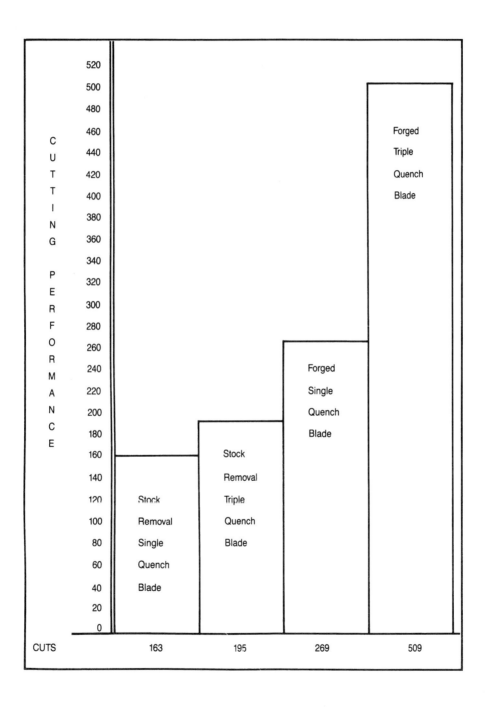

Bronzed Blades And The Multiple Quench

The more time I spend experimenting with the 'bronzing' of wire Damascus blades the firmer my conviction becomes that wire Damascus may just possibly be one of the finest potential knife materials available to the Damascus knife enthusiast. During the past four years, I have conducted countless experiments, experienced a lot of failures, hauled a lot of scrap to the dump. The net result of these efforts (of obsession may be a better word) is that I now have more questions and ideas than I ever thought possible and more importantly have been able to increase the cutting ability of the wire Damascus blade significantly over my first wire Damascus knives. This article is being written for the primary purpose of hoping to generate more interest in the Wire Damascus blade in the hopes of ending up with more folks sharing information and advancing the knifemakers search for the holly grail of knifemaking—namely the "ultimate blade material." We will probably not live to try the perfect blade, I just hope that it involves forges, hammers and anvils.

At this point I feel that there is more to the 'bronzed blade' than we will ever know. The variables are astronomical and only our budgets and imagination limit potential. I feel that wire Damascus is permeable to various elements and compounds at higher temperatures, say 1,600 to 2,300° This allows us the opportunity to develop our own alloys in fairly unsophisticated environments (the bladesmiths's shop). One process that is easily within our ability is that of 'bronzing', or more correctly **BRAZE WELDING**. Braze welding is defined as " a group of welding processes wherein the filler metal is a non-ferrous metal or alloy whose melting point is higher than 1,000°, but lower than that of the metals or alloys to be joined." I feel the 'bronzing' of wire Damascus blades with various alloys changes the steel through the alloying of the steel itself.

To date I have tried 'bronzing' wire Damascus with the following materials: Nickel; Source, Weldco alloy No. 17 containing 10% nickel, 50 % copper. This blade was about as pretty as they come, but was only at best mediocre when it came to cutting ability.

Oxygen Bearing copper: Source, copper wire. This blade would not cut rope, it would cut wood fairly well.

Bronze: Source Weldco brass rod, containing Mn .04, Cu 58% Sn .86 %, Fe .80%, Zn - balance.

Using the Welco brass rod, the following system provided the greatest level of success thus far.

My standard method of making my billet of wire Damascus was employed at the start. Eleven pieces of 9/16-inch union wire rope, improved plow, 12 inches long were forge-welded into a billet of steel. From this billet, blades were forged and the following system of bronzing hardening and tempering was employed. The blades were forged to shape, except that they were forged no thinner than 1/8 of an inch.*

Here are two of Ed's latest designs.

The blade was then heated slightly above the point of decallesence and placed in a bucket of vermiculite to cool slowly, this is a process known as annealing.

* I feel that thinning blades any further than this results in an edge that very probably has lost some of its carbon during forging,

The blades were then forged to shape. At this point they are at least 1/8-inch thick at the thinnest point. I feel that thinning blades any thinner than 1/8th inch at this time results in an edge on the finished knife that may be lower in carbon than necessary, due to carbon being burned out of the steel at forging, bronzing, hardening and tempering heats.

Next the blades are then flat ground, then hollow ground. The hollow grinding is solely for the purpose of providing an area for the brass; only the area of the blade that is to be hardened is hollow ground. This provides an area for the brass to remain on the area to be hardened, thus protecting that portion of the blade from loss of carbon during the following multiple quench.

I then bronze the surface of the blades three at a time, using a commercial brazing flux. I flow the brass onto one side then the other of each blade, taking my time and carefully ensuring that the entire hollow ground area is filled with brass, including a coat of brass on the area that will be the cutting edge. Once all three blades have been coated with brass, I increase the heat provided by the torch and keep the blades heated to the flow temp of the brass for ten minutes. (Note I always maintain a slightly excess acetylene flame, heating the blade to the point that every now and then zinc can be see burning out of the brass. (NOTE): Adequate ventilation and eye protection are mandatory; if in doubt, ask your welding supplier. Brass will flow over the entire surface of the blade;

Here the author (left) poses with Wayne Goddard. He is holding his Damascus blade, having just passed the performance section of the ABS master smith test.

that is OK, as excess will be ground off. Just be sure that you get a thorough coating over the hollow ground are as well as the edge.

Next, grind the excess brass off of the portion of the blade that is not hollow-ground, smooth up any high points of brass on the hollow ground area and inspect to make sure you have the entire area to be hardened well covered with brass. I feel that the brass protects the blade from the loss of carbon during hardening as well as continues to supply copper to the blade during hardening.

I then preheat Brownell's Trough Quench oil to 140° F. Heat the bronzed area of the blade to the point of decallessence (point where the steel looses its magnetism). I always check this point with a magnet. Hold the blade at this temperature for at least one minute. Avoid heating the blade over this point. My best results are manifest when I maintain the heat very close to the point where the magnetism attraction just ceases. An adequate flame is better than one that is too hot.

The three blades are individually quenched. At first only the hollow ground area is submerged in the oil, then when the cherry-red color is completely out of the back of the blade, the entire blade is submerged into the oil. I leave the blades in the oil till the temperature of the oil is down to 70°. The blades are then removed and a second then third quench is accomplished in the same manner as the first sequence.

The three blades are then placed in a tempering oven and triple drawn at 325° F for one hour each draw. From this point on, treat the blade like any other wire Damascus blade. Grind the brass off, grind the blade, taking off about 1/16 inch off of the cutting edge and sharpen and test the blade.

How does the triple quenched bronzed wire Damascus blades cut? My old method of bronzing wire Damascus blades resulted in blades that cut nearly as well as my old single quenched 5160 blades. These blades usually cut as well as my triple quench 5160 blades. This is outstanding performance. I feel that leaving the brass on the blades through the hardening and tempering process allows more time for the oxygen free copper to flow into the blade, as well as protecting the blade from losing carbon.

How to Freeze Quench Your Steel

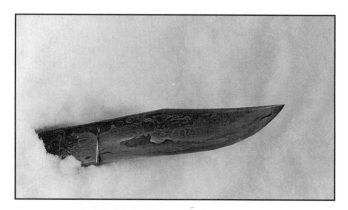

The author's chain-saw Damascus blade prior to the liquid nitrogen quench.

Whenever I see anything different, I think about making a knife out of it. Rick Dunkerley knew that and he couldn't have brought me a better gift. Rick came to my shop to share some time making, talking and experimenting with knives. He is an excellent bladesmith dedicated to making high-performance blades. Along with him he brought some of the biggest chain-saw chain I've ever seen.

He and I devoted several days to exploring new ideas, then started making chain-saw Damascus. My 150-lb. Beaudry power hammer with its flat dies is just right for making large Damascus billets. Usually a knifemaker does most of his work alone. The two of us working together kept it interesting. We put in some long hours that went fast thanks to good company. When Rick headed back to Montana, we each had a billet of chain-saw Damascus and some other experimental material that you will read about in future issues of Blade magazine.

I like to make a few Damascus knives every now and then. Damascus knives can be beautiful. I find making them challenging and rewarding. Chain-saw Damascus is one of my favorite steels to work. The only trouble with most Damascus knives I have tested is that they usually don't cut very well when compared to high-performance steel like 52100E.

One of my goals as a knifemaker has been to make Damascus that can cut with other high-performance knives I have tested. I have made some Damascus blades that cut fairly well, but they were too brittle to qualify as high-performance blades because they failed the 90° flex test. The chain-saw chain that Rick gave me was stamped Oregon on every other link. The chain's makers are obviously proud of their product. I have been told that Oregon TM chain-saw chain is some of the best. The individual links of Rick's chain measured 1-1/2 inches long. I felt that the size of the individual links might make this steel a little different when welded up into a Dam-

ascus knife. I decided to try a few different techniques and give my new Damascus a chance to enter the world of high performance knives.

I forged a blade and then applied some of the new methods that I have been using with 52100E. After normalizing, I annealed the blade three times by heating it to non-magnetic temperature, holding that temperature for two hours, then letting it cool for six hours in my Paragon oven. This was accomplished over a period of three days.

I rough ground and heated the blade to where it was just non-magnetic, then quenched it in Brownell's Tough Quench pre-heated to 165° F. Tough Quench is a fast-quench oil that is well suited to Damascus and other low carbon steels. The blade cooled to room temperature in the oil and I heated and quenched the blade a second time. (Author's note: The two quenches are less than the three quenches I use with 52100E.) I then tempered the blade three times at 350° F, allowing it to cook for two hours each time, and then cooled it slowly to room temperature in the oven.

I finished grinding the blade, sharpened it and tested it for edge toughness. The edge flexed, demonstrating excellent toughness. Rope cutting tests resulted in exceptional performance for Damascus (an average of 88 cuts), placing this

The author flexes the blade. Note his safety glasses.

After hardening and tempering the blade, the author prepares it for the liquid nitrogen bath. When working with liquid nitrogen, use care, wear safety glasses and gloves, and work outside or with good ventilation. Read the brochure, ask questions from your supplier and you should be OK.

blade as one of the better cutting Damascus blades I have tested. Now to see if the blade would flex to 90 degrees without breaking.

The Liquid Nitrogen Quench

The above procedures are nothing out of the ordinary. I have used them for years on most of my Damascus. The following procedures are something I hadn't done before.

Dick Iiams is a good friend and a fine knifemaker. He forges blades of 52100 and is dedicated to making high performance using knives. He has been using a liquid nitrogen blade quench for some time. Dick told me that when he started using multiple annealing heats on his blades, the blades responded favorably to the liquid nitrogen quench.

I decided to try a liquid nitrogen quench on my chain-saw Damascus blade. Wanting to know what the grain structure and pattern looked like, I first polished the blade, then etched it in ferric chloride. I was pleased with the resulting pattern and proceeded to hunt up some liquid nitrogen. I

called the folks at Gases Plus who keep me supplied in welding rod, oxygen and acetylene. Dennis Crowley runs the Riverton, Wyoming, store. I told him about my experiment and he loaned me a cylinder filled with liquid nitrogen. Along with the cylinder, Dennis gave me a bulletin that explained what liquid nitrogen is all about.

Safety Considerations

Liquid nitrogen is an inert gas. There are some important safety rules to follow but its use is much simpler than I thought.

Liquid nitrogen is -320°F. If you spill it, it will freeze anything it touches. Warning: It won't poison you but you can't survive breathing it. Use care, wear safety glasses and gloves, and work outside or with good ventilation. Read the brochure, ask questions from your supplier and you should be OK.

I drilled a small hole in the tang of the chain-saw Damascus blade and fastened a handle on it using bailing wire. I submerged the blade in the cylinder of liquid nitrogen and let it soak for four hours. After four hours I removed the blade and placed it in vermiculite to let the blade warm slowly. (Author's note: Professional heat treater Paul Bos recommends a tempering heat after the blade has been quenched in liquid nitrogen. I didn't know that at the time, so this blade did not receive a final tempering heat.)

I sharpened the blade on my Norton India fine-grit bench stone and checked the edge for toughness by flexing it over a steel. The edge flexed and returned to where it was supposed to with ease edge toughness at its best! The blade averaged 180 cuts, which was nearly twice as many as before the freeze quench. Sharpening the blade between cutting tests was delightful; it was still extremely easy to sharpen.

There are four basic qualities in a using knife of paramount importance. The knife must cut, be strong, easy to sharpen and, last but not least, be tough. Once a piece of steel

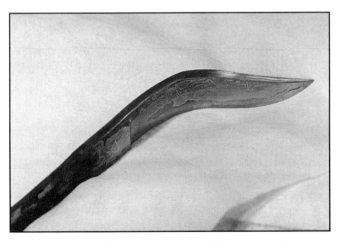

After being flexed more than 90°, the blade partially sprang back to straight.

The author said the freeze-quenched blade cut better than any Damascus blade he's ever tested.

has these traits, the maker can make a quality knife. If a blade lacks these traits, no amount of engraving, money, workmanship, fancy handle material or good intentions on the part of the maker can fix it. Cover a poor performing blade with chocolate or diamonds and it may taste or look better, but you still have a poor performing blade.

The chain-saw Damascus blade had qualified in the first three tests. Now was time for the final test, the test of toughness that separates the great knives from the rest of the pack.

I like the toughness test that the American Bladesmith Society uses. Secured in a vise, the blade is flexed to 90°. If the knife doesn't break, it is a good blade provided that it cuts. All that remained for the blade to meet my standards for a high-performance using knife was to flex 90° without breaking, cracking or chipping.

I clamped the blade into the post vise in front of my shop, the vise that has witnessed many successes and failures for the past 20 years. Two pieces of wood protected the blade from the rough faces of the vise jaws. Caution: Whenever testing knife blades, be sure and wear safety glasses. Blades can snap and small pieces of them can bounce the last place you want a piece of steel is in your eye.

I slid the piece of pipe that I use for the flex test over the tang and applied pressure. The blade resisted flexing well with uniform strength throughout the test. After being flexed to 90°, it partially returned to straight. The blade had done all it needed to do.

This is only one test blade. Many more will follow before I consider the results conclusive. The test results indicate that the performance of chain-saw Damascus blades can be enhanced through the super cold treatment of liquid nitrogen. Conclusion: Wire and other Damascus steels benefit from freeze treating without significant financial outlay by the bladesmith. If you can't or don't wish to freeze quench blades yourself, a number of professionals such as Paul Bos will do it at a reasonable cost.

Follow-Up: Freeze Treating 5160

The frozen blade was strong and flexed to 90° without cracking.

After the success I experienced with freeze treating chain-saw Damascus in the June "Blade," I was anxious to continue the experiments with other steels. First on the list: 5160. I have a special love for the 5160. It was one of the first steels I forged, one that is especially responsive to forging and multiple-quench heat treatments. The 5160 steel is widely used by a number of bladesmiths, is readily available and is quite versatile. what's more, another knifemaker, Randy Strickland, reported increased strength in his 5160 blades after freezing them in liquid nitrogen.

As a source of steel for the test knives, I used a 1-1/8-inch round bar of steel that had served as a rock shaft in a John Deere tractor. Used John Deere shafts are a reliable, inexpensive source for extremely clean, high-grade 5160. I forged two blades form the bar stock. After forging, I normalized them by heating them to critical temperature (determined by testing with a magnet) and allowing them to air cool to room temperature. I then annealed both blades three times by heating them to critical temperature and allowing them to cool slowly to room temperature.

I obtained the first annealing heat in my Mankel Forge and the second and third annealing heats in my Paragon oven, heating them to 1440°F., holding at that temperature for two hours and then letting them cool in the over over the next six hours. Thermal cycles such as normalizing and multiple annealing are basic steps that with some steels can lead to extremely consistent, high performance blades that never warp during hardening cycles.

Following the normalizing and annealing thermal cycles, I hardened the 5160 blades in Texaco type "A" quenching oil that was preheated to 165° F. Using a Victor No. 3 tip on my oxyacetylene torch and a 3X flame, I heated the lower third of the blades until they became non-magnetic (verified by use of a magnet), and quenched the cutting edge and lower third of the blade in the heated oil. I let the blades cool to room temperature in the oil. I repeated the process twice more for a total of three hardening cycles.

Next, I tempered the blades twice in the Paragon oven by heating them to 388° F, holding at that temperature for two hours, then allowing them to cool in the oven to room temperature. These cycles required about five hours. Fellow American Bladesmith Society member, friend and knifemaker Rick Dunkerley took part in the experiment from this point forward. Together we tested a lot of knives and cut a lot of rope. Cutting rope with test blades is hard on your hand as the blades usually don't have handles and your hands have to work more. Dunkerley taped his fingers to keep the blisters he got from getting any worse. He talked about sore arms and still never lost his enthusiasm over wanting to see what was coming next. That kind of curiosity is what it takes to make great knives.

I finished grinding the blades, we sharpened them and then tested their performance abilities. I learned the following tests from Wayne Goddard's story in the December 1992 Blade (page 52). I consider it the most significant article influencing the quality control of knives ever published. Rick and I flexed the edges over a sharpening steel. When they did not chip, it indicated that they were tough. We tested their cutting ability by cutting one lay out of a 1-1/4-inch hemp rope.

The blades averaged 132 cuts over repeated tests. This performance level is somewhat better than the previous 5160 blades I had tested, probably because of the multiple annealing heats on these blades and the lack of same on the previously tested 5160 blades. Rick and I quenched the blades in liquid nitrogen (-320° F) for four hours. We removed the blades from the quench and placed them in vermiculite to warm to room temperature slowly for about two hours. (Author's note: Paul Bos recommends that a freeze treated blade should be tempered after freeze treating. I did not do so. If I did, I would temper the blades by heating them for two hours at 350° F.)

Rick Dunkerley and I flexed the edges over a sharpening steel. When they did not chip, it indicated that they were tough.

Rick and I again tested the edges for toughness by flexing them over a steel rod. The edge of both blades flexed, requiring extreme pressure, then returned to where they were supposed to be. We flexed one edge three times-right, left, then right again-with no evidence of chipping. This degree of edge strength and toughness is as good as it gets. If the edge had chipped, I would have tempered the blade again at a temperature 25° hotter that the first tempering temperature and retested the working hardness of the edge. When the edge quits chipping, you have reached the ideal working hardness level for that particular blade. Rick and I tested cutting performance on hemp rope as described previously. After the first 100 cuts, the freeze-treated blade still shaved hair!

Repeated tests of the freeze-treated blades resulted in an average of 270 cuts, a little better than double the cutting performance over the same blade before freeze treating. This is definitely high performance. The cutting edge remained crisp and would still cut paper after dulling on the ropecutting tests.

We were down to the last challenge: Would the blades flex to 180° without breaking? We tested the smaller of the two blades. We placed it in a vise, padded the vise jaws with oak blocks, slid a cheater pipe over the tang and applied pressure. The blade resisted flexing with amazing strength, requiring significantly more pressure than any blade of similar size that I have tested for flex. Of all the testing I have done, this blade holds the record for strength. The blade flexed to 90° without cracking. I continued to about 110° and it still held together! When I relaxed the flexing pressure, the blade returned to about 30°. Again, this is phenomenal performance. The results of this experiment indicate that freeze treating forged 5160 steel blades after normalizing, multiple annealing and triple-quench thermal cycles dramatically improves the cutting performance and strength of the blade.

I have tested freeze-treated blades before and they did not perform as well as these blades did. Why? I feel that over the years my forging techniques have improved considerably. I pay strict attention to the temperature of the steel I am working. I don't allow interruptions to distract me that result in overheated blades. Each individual thermal treatment is as important as any other event in the development of the finished knife.

When seeking combinations of materials and techniques that may produce high-performance blades, everything that happens to that steel may significantly influence the finished product. High-performance blades are the result of doing everything right. Anything that you do to a piece of steel must be carefully thought out and accomplished for a reason.

In this experiment, 5160 blades forged from a recycled, 1-1/8-inch round bar and subjected to specific thermal treatments demonstrated enhanced cutting performance and strength after being subjected to a four-hour cooling cycle in liquid nitrogen at -320° F. Testing on the remaining blade and some future blades will continue and you will read about these experiments in coming issues of "Blade."

Blades From Ball Bearings: The 52100 Solution

Introduction

Wayne Goddard first introduced me to the idea that 52100 E steel could make a truly high performance knife. He sent me ball bearings, asked me about working them every time we talked and kept me seeking an acceptable blade made from one. Thanks Wayne!

What is it about a ball bearing that keeps my attention so focused? I love them, that is all there is to it. I believe that this love affair started when I was a little kid playing with marbles. My 'steely, was by far my favorite, even more so than the 'agates' my grandfather gave me. As time went on my fascination with them grew. When working on equipment, I always saved old ball bearings and put them in those special places that every shop has.

Civilization as we know it from the industrial revolution until now and into the future in one way or another rides, works, flies, cooks, eats, sleeps, heats and cools through the contribution of ball bearings. I never get bored looking into a ball bearing looking for knives to be made for many knife blades live together in a three inch ball bearing just waiting to be liberated and join the world of knives. Ball bearings, one of the miracles of man, how senseless to let them go to scrap.

Special note from the author: I didn't intend to write this article this soon. I am writing it now because 52100 is becoming a popular steel and is not available to knifemakers in ready-to-forge form. Makers have to develop their billets from finished products like ball bearings and bearing races. Trouble is, there is a very important safety precaution you must take before developing a billet from a hardened piece of steel. Namely, the steel MUST be annealed (softened) before any welding is done on it. A new knifemaker recently called me and complained that a ball bearing that he had welded to a bar prior to forging had exploded. Fortunately, no one was hurt. I have never witnessed a ball bearing that was being welded explode, but I have heard about it happening enough from reputable sources that I felt I should let you know how to develop 52100 into a usable form safely.

I demand three levels of performance from any knife intended for serious use. First, it must have the ability to cut and cut well. Second, the blade must be tough. By tough I mean it must flex without breaking like a piece of glass. Last, but not least, it must be relatively easy to sharpen. Through the years, I have tried many steels and heat-treating methods and have tested the results by cutting a lot of rope and breaking many blades. Some combinations have cut extremely well, but have

broken or chipped when subjected to hard use. Drawn to a point where they were tough, these blades were too soft to cut effectively. I had settled upon one steel that when properly forged and heat treated cut very well. I had invested a great amount of time and effort getting the most out of that steel, so I was reluctant to change.

My friend and fellow knifemaker, Wayne Goddard, had been challenging me to try some steels he said were superior to mine. Wayne twisted my arm and bent my ear for several years. I had tried other steels and didn't get the performance I was getting from my old favorite steel. It is pretty hard to change from something that works. It's kind of like buying a new hat; things just don't seem to fit.

Three 3-inch-diameter ball bearings. The ball on the left is as they are usually found-rusting and waiting for some loving attention. The middle ball has been cleaned and polished. The ball on the right has been etched in ferric chloride to reveal the grain structure of the steel. Light buffing usually helps determine grain flow. Arrows drawn on the ball indicate an average grain flow.

I started to doubt my choice of knife steel when Wayne showed me a knife he had forged from a ball bearing (52100 steel). He had etched the blade in ferric chloride (Archer Etchant, available at Radio Shack stores) and the visible grain structure was absolutely beautiful. Not only was the blade beautiful, it was flawless and cut exceptionally well. I decided that it could be well worth my time and effort to develop a forging and heat-treating process for 52100 steel. I didn't complete many knives for several months, but the results were well worth it.

Using bearing-quality 52100 steel for knives offers a significant advantage. The quality control governing the manufacture and selection of bearing-quality 52100 steel is rigid,

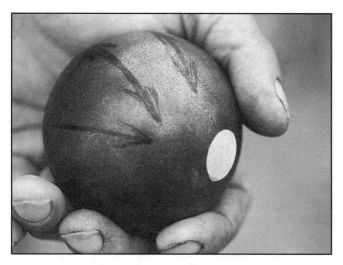

Once you determine the grain flow of the steel, grind a flat spot on the ball on one end of the grain flow or the other. This is where you weld a bar to the ball after the ball has been heated in order to anneal (soften) the ball. Forget this step and you must again determine the direction of the grain flow since the arrows will burn off during heating.

Weld the ball to a bar, heat to forging temperature and you are ready to reduce the ball to a manageable steel billet.

Next, heat the ball to a dull red and let it cool slowly. This anneals the ball and you can then weld a bar of steel on to it, providing a handle to facilitate forging. This is probably the most important step thus far because welding anything to a hardened ball bearing or race can cause the hardened steel to shatter, sometimes violently. CAUTION: NEVER WELD ON A HARDENED BEARING BALL OR RACE. ALWAYS ANNEAL THEM YOURSELF BEFORE WELDING. DON'T TAKE ANYONE'S WORD FOR IT. ANNEAL IT YOURSELF FIRST!

Start by forging the ball into a square block...

producing top-quality steel. The etching of blades reveals faults you won't normally see in a polished blade. I have etched all of my 52100 steel blades and have yet to find any faults in them.

The main problem (spelled "opportunity") is that there is no economical source for 52100 steel available to knifemakers other than from used steel. Ball and roller bearings and bearing races are the best source of 52100. Developing a billet of steel from these sources is easy when you know how. Here's how I've been forging used bearing quality steel into billets to be forged into knife blades:

Locating usable ball and roller bearings is the first hurdle. Bearings are everywhere but most of them are too little for anything heavier than smaller blades. Larger-sized bearings are used in oil-well drilling rigs, crushers, drag lines and some heavy equipment. Once you find bearings of adequate

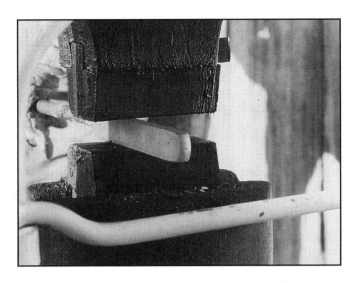

...then work the square into a rectangular bar. The author uses flattening dies. Keep the steel hot; when it quits moving under the power hammer, go back to the forge and reheat it.

size (they may have names and numbers stamped on them), you can usually determine the type of steel used in them by simply contacting a bearing supplier. Bearings named "Fafnir," "SKF" and "FAG" are usually made of 52100.

You will also find bearings made of stainless steel, probably 440C, M-50 and some steels that you can't anneal and others that won't harden. Some roller bearings are mild steel that has been case hardened. If you find these, save them for making Damascus steel. If the bearing steel you select will rust, sparks when you grind it and hardens when you quench it, it is probably 52100.

Forging a knife blade from a large ball or roller bearing allows you to work the steel extensively. Steel that has been forged extensively tends to respond to sophisticated heat treatment, producing a significantly better blade when compared to a blade that required a minimal amount of forging.

At first the search for 52100 steel can be frustrating. You will receive lots of advice from folks who have never made a knife, and you may experience some disappointments. If you stick with it, you will make a knife using top-quality steel on which you can count. You will also command a better understanding of what bladesmithing is all about.

Caution: Welding on hardened steel such as a ball bearing can result in internal stresses created when the weld cools. These stresses can cause the hardened steel to shatter, sometimes violently. Annealing the hardened bearing-quality steel or simply heating it to a dull red color prior to welding prevents stresses from developing.

Forging The Fowler Way Part 1:
The Trick Is To Forge It Thick

Before heat treating, grind off all hammer marks, establish the ricasso grind line and remove all scratches with a 300-grit finish.

When it comes to forging blades, there seems to be some special accolades for those who can forge a blade exactly to shape. This is the mark of a true forged blade, or so they say. However, there's more to a high-performance blade than simply forging it to shape.

Years ago, I remember forging with another bladesmith in a shop a thousand miles from home. He came to forge steel carrying a black leather case, much like a doctor would bring on a house call. Out of the case he took a sheepskin roll similar to the knife rolls the pocketknife folks carry. He carefully and slowly unrolled what proved to be some of the most highly polished hammers I've ever seen. I figured right away that he knew a whole lot more about forging than I did. Had I not been so intimidated by his manner and paraphernalia, I would have taken some pictures.

I felt kind of bashful as I took my prized homemade, secondhand hammer out of my suitcase. I looked at its bruised face and taped handle and felt like I was in the wrong place. I kept it hidden and put off forging a blade myself so I wouldn't appear too far afield. I decided to watch him and try to learn what he knew that I didn't.

I observed him at work and it wasn't long before I wasn't nearly as impressed as I had been at the time of his glorious entrance. He spent hours working over a blade, a lot of time heating it in the coal forge, sometimes timidly hammering on the blade to be, obviously more afraid of hurting his hammers than making a knife. After each forging episode, he spent time cleaning his hammers and worrying about any marks on their highly polished faces. His work progressed painfully and slowly. The blade he forged was right down to a gnat's eyebrow when he finished. Very little grinding was required

(or was possible due to the thin blade) to finish the knife. The only trouble with the blade was that there was probably very little carbon left in the steel, most of it having been burned out in the fire.

There are as many ways of forging a blade as there are bladesmiths. Some start with a piece of steel approximating the dimensions of the finished blade, heat it up, give it a few swats with a hammer and call it a forged blade. The bladesmith who starts with the largest piece of steel he can handle and carefully works it down to the shape he wants has the potential to make a better knife.

The question is, how far, or how close to the finished blade, should the blade smith forge the steel?

At one time, it was believed that forged blades needed to be used and sharpened several times before they started cutting to their maximum potential. I pondered this concept for

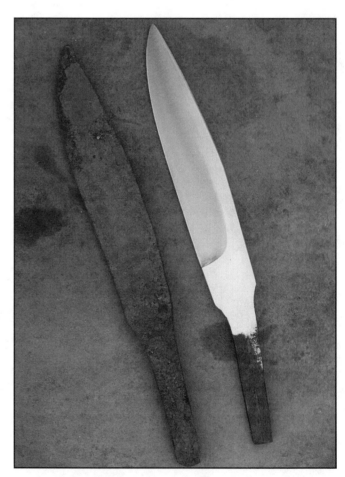

The piece at right has been profiled and ground to the approximate final geometry 1/16 inch oversize. The blade at left is just as it was forged.

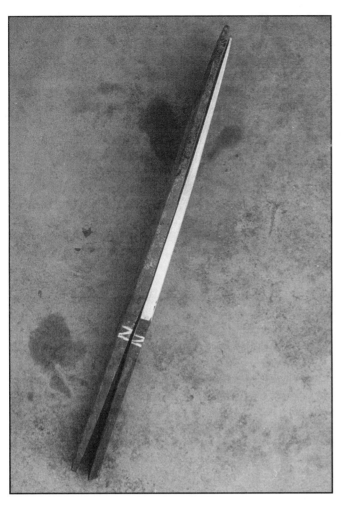

An overhead view of the two blades. Note how much thicker the unground forged blade is.

awhile. I couldn't see how using and sharpening a blade would "break it in" there had to be something else influencing blade performance. It didn't take too many experiments to determine that the blade that was closely forged to shape and then hardened and tempered needed to be ground back to reveal the higher performing steel hidden inside the outer shell.

Maximum Performance

For blades that cut to the steel's maximum performance level, the bladesmith should start with the largest steel he/she can handle, forge the blade oversize by at least 3/16-inch, then grind off all the steel that was exposed to the fire during the forging process, removing all evidence of hammer marks. Then, in preparing the steel for hardening, profile the blade geometry about 1/16-inch oversize on each side, thus enveloping the finished blade with enough steel to protect it from carbon loss during the heat-treating process to come.

Final preparation for heat treating consists of grinding all scratches from the blade to a 300-grit finish and rounding all sharp edges, including the cutting edge, This is necessary because any hammer pits or scratches on the blade surface during the hardening process may be responsible for blade failures that sometimes defy any other explanation.

By starting with a larger piece of steel and forging it to shape oversize, the bladesmith can capitalize on the qualities developed in the steel by virtue of the forging process. Then, he/she can grind off all the surface steel that was in actuality simply used to manipulate the steel inside to make a better knife. Forge the blade oversize, grind down to clean steel, then finish the blade with a 300-grit belt. These methods leave the bladesmith plenty of steel with which to work, as well as protect the finished blade from carbon loss during the heat-treating process. After the hardening and tempering procedure, the best of the blade will lie 1/16-inch inside the outer shell, and that 1/16-inch can be ground off during the final finishing.

Forging The Fowler Way Part II:
Elements of Basic Forging

The author hammers steel in his Wyoming shop.

Forging a blade exactly to shape is a skill that should be mastered by every bladesmith. Over a period of time, he/she will develop the ability to manipulate the steel using a hammer with grace, precision and efficiency. Developing this ability to a fine degree is definitely an art.

"Precision forging" also results in thrifty and conservative use of blade materials. There was a time in the history of bladesmithing when first-rate high carbon steel was an extremely rare and valuable asset. The bladesmith who could squeeze a few more blades out of a pound of steel was economically ahead of the competition.

While being able to forge a blade exactly to shape is an admirable skill which enhances the economical use of blade materials, there's a whole lot more to a high-performance blade than forging a blade to shape just to try to save a few pennies. While I don't deny the importance of the blade-

smith's ability to forge a blade exactly to shape, I do strongly feel that there's more to the development of a truly high-performance blade than simply forging to exact shape. Today's bladesmith lives in the land of plenty. Top-quality high carbon steel is readily available and the cost of materials is an insignificant fraction of the value of the time the bladesmith will devote to a high-performance knife.

Precision forging or forging down to nearly the exact shape of the blade is not only unnecessary, it's also detrimental to the qualities of the finished piece. While manipulation, by forging, can improve the internal quality of the steel, the qualities imparted to the inner steel must be at the sacrifice of the outer shell. By forging oversize, the outer shell can be ground away, leaving the finished blade with the highest-quality steel possible. (For more on this principle, see "The Trick Is To Forge It Thick" in the April *Blade*.)

The fine flakes indicate the steel was forged at a lower temperature more conducive to a high-performance blade.

The potential qualities of some steels are actually enhanced by the degree of properly accomplished forging prior to the heat-treating process. Simply put, the more you work it the better it gets, provided it's forged steel done right!

Methods And Theories

Forging a blade can be accomplished in many ways. Gas, coal or electricity can power forges. The heat source isn't nearly as critical to developing the high-performance blade as the dedication, ability and knowledge of the bladesmith. The old adages, "strike while the steel is hot," "don't get too many irons in the fire" and "tend the fire carefully" are well known to bladesmiths who seek excellence in their knives.

The heated steel can be formed through the use of hydraulic presses, power hammers or the tried-and-true hand-held hammer and anvil. Again, the quality of the finished blade depends on the skill, dedication and methods of bladesmiths much more so than the tools they use.

There are rules, theories and practical methods that I apply to forging a blade. First my theory, based on what I've read, heard from those who should know and my own experience making and testing blades. The more you work a piece of steel with heat and mechanical force, the greater the potential for a high-performance blade, provided you know what you're doing and dedicate all your abilities to each and every blade you make. While forging a blade, it's absolutely mandatory that you pay close attention to the birth of that blade.

Overheating the steel or working it too cold are some of the unforgivable errors waiting to be made. Work the steel too cold and it will crack, resulting in an obviously defective blade. Overheating can result in a defective piece of lesser quality that may pass visual inspection but that's potentially more detrimental to the reputation of the forged blade because its faults are not always readily apparent. This is but one reason why a blade forged by an experienced and dedicated bladesmith can be more reliable than one forged by the novice or smith who's more concerned with quantity than quality. The best blades come from the smith who walks a tightrope, carefully balancing the correct temperature and mechanical force, and efficiently working the steel within the forging process.

The Steel

Some steels are more forgiving than others. Best for the beginning bladesmith is 5160. It's a great confidence builder and, as you work it, you can learn a lot, if you pay attention. The biggest problem with that last statement is that it takes a lot of learning to know what the focus of your attention should be. Time, dedication, curiosity and testing your finished product are the best paths to success. I could easily look up some empirical data and state what the correct forging temperatures are for any particular steel. The only problem with such information is that it will mean little or nothing to you while you're forging a blade.

The bladesmith must rely on obvious and predictable indicators of temperature while working in the shop. The guidelines that I use to indicate the correct forging temperature are readily apparent to the eye that wishes to know. When I remove a piece of steel from the heat of the forge and see thick sheets of scale forming on the future blade, I know that the steel is too hot. My "personal gauge" to the proper high end of the forging temperature registers when only light scale forms due to the temperature and resulting oxidation of the steel. This phenomenon is easily observed as you work the blade with your hammer. I like to see light, tiny flakes of scale coming off the future blade. The scale flakes should resemble powdered snow on your anvil, easily blown off with your breath.

As long as the steel keeps moving due to the force of your hammer, keep working it. As the steel cools, you'll notice your progress toward the shaped blade slowing down. Before the steel starts ringing like a bell or bouncing from the hammer blows, it's time to return it to the heat of the forge. Simply stated, when it quits moving, quit hitting.

Use the above guidelines a few times and you'll be forging at the correct temperature and recognizing the telltale colors of the steel in your shop, night or day, when you're within the forging range of that steel. Consistent top-quality, high-performance blades are the result of the bladesmith's dedication to paying attention to temperature and walking that narrow line to perfection.

(Author's note: The preceding discussion pertains to 5160 and 52100 steels. Other steels may or may not conform to these guidelines.)

Forging The Fowler Way Part III:
How To Forge A Blade

Once you've worked the steel down to a manageable size for the desired blade shape, forge the tip.

My preferred steel is 52100, obtained from 3-inch-diameter ball bearings. I've been criticized for wasting time working blades from this size of stock. I don't consider it unnecessary labor but an opportunity to work the steel as much as possible to capitalize on the benefits of the forging process.

As many beginning bladesmiths don't have access to a power hammer large enough to work down a piece of steel of the aforementioned size, for the purpose of this discussion I will use a load shaft from a John Deere tractor. Made from 5160, such shafts consistently have provided me with high quality steel. I've never found any defects in used load shafts, which are readily available from most John Deere dealers. Since mechanics hate to throw away a good piece of steel, there's usually an ample supply of load shafts around the repair shop. These are often available for the cost of a couple dozen doughnuts come coffee time.

Even should you be forced to buy a new John Deere load shaft, one of the larger ones costs around $100 brand new and should produce 10-to-15 blades. Considering the quality of the steel, this isn't an excessive price to pay. Still, I'd probably drive another 100 miles to find a used one.

Load shafts are round bars and enable the bladesmith to work the steel to a greater degree than when starting with flat stock. If you can't find round stock, start with the largest flat stock you're able to work down. To control the bar stock while forging it, weld on a handle of 3/4-inch-round bar stocks about three feet long. Use anything that can take the heat and provide enough mass to do the job. Trying to hold a hot piece of steel with a pair of tongs is more aggravation than it's worth.

Once you've welded the bar stock to the handle, heat the billet and start working it down into a flat bar. I use dies in my power hammers that are almost flat, having just a trace of a curve in them. The use of such dies enables me to work the steel under the hammer in order to develop the greatest potential benefit from forging. When working down a billet of steel, always balance your hammer blows. Work each side of the billet the same; hit on one side, turn it over and do the same. Working in a billet in this manner develops a uniform grain flow and a better blade.

When you decide on the blade length, mark the area where the tang will begin.

Shaping Up

Once the steel is worked down to a manageable size for the desired blade shape (as measured by an experienced eye), forge the tip. Many times I've watched smiths try to make a blade by forging the tang first. This causes more trouble than it's worth. Remember: Forge the point of the blade first and you'll avoid many problems that can occur later in the forging process.

Once you've forged the tip of the blade, forge the tapers in the blade from back to tip and spine to cutting edge. Remember to forge the blade oversize 1) to allow for grinding out all hammer marks and 2) to remove steel that loses carbon during heat-treating. Leave at least 3/6 of an inch of steel at the cutting edge prior to heat-treating.

Once you've shaped the profile and tapers, you easily can make the blade longer or shorter. A little more forging from the billet, thus adding steel to the blade, will make it longer. If you have enough blade forged, simply mark it and

After shaping the tang, use the cut-off hardy to separate the blade from the billet.

Check the final blade shape one last time, using the sides and flat surfaces of the anvil as a guide,

begin forging the tang. When you decide on the blade length, mark the area where the tang will begin and forge it from the blade back to the end of the tang. Once you start forging the tang, you're committed to blade length. The only way you can make it longer is to make it thinner or narrower.

When it comes to forging the tang, use drawing dies to shape it as efficiently as possible. I prefer to taper the tang, being careful to leave enough steel for strength. The tang should never be hardened; all it has to do is be tough and strong, fairly simple requirements for steels like 5160 or 52100. Once the blade and tang are forged, straighten the blade using the straight lines along the side and face of your anvil as a guide. Due to the mass supporting the blade, it's easier to fine tune the blade while it's still attached to the billet than it will be later.

For years I cut the blade from the billet and then tried to fine-tune the blade shape. I can't count how many hot blades I picked up off the floor after they spun out of the tongs. After shaping the tang, use the cutoff hardy to separate the blade from the billet. Check the blade once more for straightness and do any fine tuning that's necessary.

Forging the Fowler Way Part IV:
Normalizing & Annealing

To normalize blades, heat them to the non-magnetic temperature and place them where they can cool in still air (here in the author's aluminum channel) to room temperature.

Once the blade is forged and straightened, I again place it in the forge until it reaches the temperature where it's just non-magnetic. I then place it in an aluminum rack and allow it to cool in still air. This process is known as normalizing.

Note: Always use a magnet to validate your perception of steel temperature by color. If you rely solely on color, you're headed for mistakes. Color perception varies with time of day, the light source in your shop and your physical condition. When it comes to normalizing 5160 and 52100, as soon as either becomes non-magnetic, you've achieved the correct temperature.

Don't ever hurry the normalizing process. "Tincture of time" is one of the most essential elements of the high-performance blade. No matter what, let the blade cool to room temperature before doing anything else to it. Don't try to hurry this step. Believe it or not, a lot that seems to influence the development of the high-performance blade happens during this stage.

Years ago I was involved in some experiments and was so enthusiastic with the outcome that I didn't let the blades cool slowly enough. I "normalized them fast." My seemingly simple shortcut made the results of the experiments that followed misleading. In short, I wasted weeks by saving a few hours.

Bladesmith's Anneal

Recently I've extended the normalizing process to something I call a Multiple Bladesmith's Anneal. The procedure is a cross between an actual textbook annealing cycle and the normalizing cycle discussed above. Since the forge is still hot following the forging of a blade, after the blade has completed the normalizing cycle (cooling to room temperature), I simply return it edge up into the forge. I turn the forge off and allow it to cool to room temperature. This normally takes about seven hours in my well-insulated Mankel three-burner forge.

The next day (day two), I place the blade in my Paragon oven, set the oven to heat to 1,440' F in one hour, then hold that heat for two hours and shut it off. Again, I allow the oven to cool to room temperature. On day three, I repeat the process of day two. Many times I take the cycle a little deeper by placing the blades in the freezer between cycles. While the freezer stage may or may not be necessary, I do it because a) it doesn't hurt the blade and b) it might help it.

Always tend the blade close while heating it in the forge. Overheating the steel can harm the quality of the finished knife.

Previous to using the Multiple Bladesmith's Anneal, during testing I found that the best blades, on occasion, out cut the poorest blades by about 10 percent. Now, all my blades consistently cut exceptionally well with very few significant individual differences. I feel that the Multiple Bladesmith's Anneal definitely reduces individual differences

123

between blades. It also makes the development of a hardening and tempering process, finely tuned to the particular steel, much more feasible to the bladesmith using 5160 and 52100.

Another process that seems to lead to high-performance blades is to randomly quench them in quenching oil during the forging process. The random quench consists of submerging a blade at forging temperature in quenching oil until the color is out of the blade (as opposed to the hardening process, the temperature of the oil at this time doesn't seem to be a significant factor). Then, return the blade to the heat of the forge and proceed with the forging.

I stumbled on this method by accident. Thinner aspects of the blade heat up faster in the forge than the thicker aspects. In order to prevent overheating the thin areas, I cooled them in oil for a short time, then returned the blade to the forge for the rest of it to reach the desired temperature. Wondering if any negative results manifested themselves in the finished blade, I purposely quenched a blade many times during the forging process, then compared it to a blade that received no quenches during forging.

Both blades were treated exactly the same after forging, receiving the Multiple Bladesmith's Anneal, and then multiple quenched and tempered three times at the same temperature. The blade that received the quenches during forging was much tougher than the blade that wasn't quenched. They both cut about the same.

A further benefit of using the Multiple Bladesmith's Anneal is that since I started using the process, none of the blades, no matter how long, thick, etc., have warped during the hardening and tempering cycles that follow.

Conclusion

There's a lot more information that could have been added to the material discussed here. For example, an entire book could be written on the subject of hammers alone. I've tried to limit the information to the most basic and most frequently misunderstood elements of the forged blade. Most of what you've read here, if applied to forged blades, won't make them look any better. "Cosmetic knives" are another issue entirely. The only blades that interest me are those that cut, are strong and tough, and can be relied on in a pinch.

The smith who sells his blades under the guise of using knives should devote all his efforts to making the best using blade possible. Once he's pushed his steel of choice to the limit and achieves truly high-performance knives on a regular basis, he can cover them with any tinsel he wishes.

The sad fact of our times is that most of those who seek the Excalibur of today will never be in a position to put the knife to the ultimate test. Still, bladesmiths need to inform the consumer of the true nature of their knives. It's the obligation of smiths proclaiming to produce the high-performance blade to constantly seek perfection in their work. In all probability, only the bladesmith who makes the knife will know the potential of the blade. Still, the smith with a conscience, governed by ethics, will always stand on the frontier of the forged blade, seeking the ultimate level of performance.

52100 From A Metallurgist's View

Usually, the only testing available to individual knife-makers involves simple, but reliable, cutting and torture tests of blades. From the results of these tests some believe that blades forged from 52100 steel can reach extremely high levels of performance. While these tests define 52100 on the basis of performance, skeptics of the forged blade in general and 52100 in particular-question the reliability of these procedures and suggest the need for verification in the form of professional analysis.

Now, thanks to Metallographic Laboratory Services [2610 Old First St., Livermore, CA 94550 (510) 455-9602] and the help of ABS master smith Rick Dunkerley, there's data that empirically describes the physical properties of blades forged, shaped and enhanced by simple but extremely effective physical and thermal treatments.

The Method

The blades for this experiment were forged from virgin 52100E of 1-inch-round bar stock. The temperature of the steel was carefully controlled by using the bladesmith's eye and tending the steel closely. Flat dies were used in order to work the steel as much as possible. While forging, the heated blades were edge quenched three times in room temperature Conoco paraffin quenching oil (the same as Texaco Type "A" quenching oil). This is a slow quench medium that is essentially a heavy mineral oil. The quenches were performed randomly during the forging process. The blades were then heated to the point where they were non-magnetic and allowed to air cool in the thermal treatment known as normalizing.

Again heated to non-magnetic and allowed to cool in vermiculite, the blades required about six hours to cool. This process was repeated three times over a period of three days. Convex ground from a 36-grit belt all the way down to a 220-grit belt, the blades were left about 3/32 inch oversize on the cutting edge. The extra steel was left in order to protect the edge from any possible carbon loss during the following thermal cycles:

The blades were again treated to three thermal cycles by heating them to nonmagnetic and allowing them to cool for 10 minutes in still air at room temperature, then repeating the process twice more. After the third heat, the blades were allowed to cool to room temperature. Rick and I feel that this process reduces the steel's grain size dramatically, allowing future thermal treatments to push the steel to its maximum potential.

The blades were then subjected to a triple quench as follows:

All the blades were heated to nonmagnetic and edge quenched in the Conoco pale paraffin oil (which had been preheated to 165° F) until all the red color was out of each one. The blades then were fully submerged in the oil and allowed to cool to room temperature for 24 hours. The hardening cycle was repeated twice more over the next two days for a total of three thermal cycles. The blades were then tempered for two hours at 375 degrees F in Rick's household oven, cooled to room temperature, then submerged in liquid nitrogen for 24 hours.

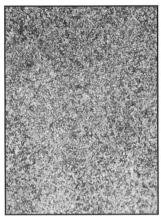 

The cutting edge of the test blade subjected to the author's thermal cycles shows very fine grain structure (left) as opposed to the larger grain structure (right) of the spine of the same blade that was never heated to critical temperature and not submerged in oil until the blade was relatively cool. (Photos at 1000X by Metallographic Laboratory Services.)

After the freeze, the blades were removed from the liquid nitrogen and allowed to warm to room temperature. They were given two more tempering cycles at 375° F for two hours each cycle, allowing the blades to cool to room temperature between cycles. The blades were then finished with a convex grind and tested for cutting and toughness.

The above procedures resulted in an increase in cutting performance of 300 percent over previous 52100E blades from virgin steel that had not been freeze treated and that could pass the following tests:

The cutting edge of the test blade easily flexed over a brass rod. One of the blades was flexed back and forth a full 180° 6 1/2 times before the edge cracked. This level of performance may seem unnecessary but exhibits the ability of the steel to withstand all any man could expect from a knife, and more.

(Author's note: Tests show that the nature of virgin 52100E steel varies slightly from 52100E obtained from used ball bearings. It will also vary from hot- rolled 52100E. The complex nature of the heat-treating requires that each bladesmith

fine-tune his methods to push the steel he uses to the limit. A source for 52100 steels of all kinds is Daryl Meier.)

Grain Structure

In order to determine the nature of the steel from a metallurgist's view, a test blade was sent to Metallographic Laboratory Services (MLS) for photographic analysis.

Sam DiGiallonardo, owner of MLS, stated that the sample had the finest grain structure in the cutting edge of any steel he had ever examined. He also stated that there was no retained austenite in the matrix that consisted of spheroidized iron and chrome carbides, tempered martensite and lower bainite. The carbide size was between one half and one micron. This is as fine as it gets (one micron is one one-thousandth of a millimeter). For comparison, carbides in D2 steel are 10 to 15 microns and CPM 440-V carbides are two to four microns in fully heat-treated blades.

The Rockwell hardness of the cutting edge was 58 RC while the spine of the blade registered a Rockwell of 30 RC.

The center of the blade was well annealed, never hardened and actually tested softer than the spine. Analysis revealed ferrite with carbides in the transition zone between the edge and spine.

Translated into knife talk for the blade enthusiast, I offer the following personal opinions: Cutting ability and toughness are firmly rooted to the nature of the crystalline structure of the edge. My previous experiments based solely on cutting performance indicate that an edge of ultra-fine crystals can outcut a harder edge of larger crystal size and still remain tougher, as well as being easier to sharpen.

These results clearly and conclusively prove that the bladesmith who's truly dedicated to developing blades that can and do stand up to hard use can accomplish superior results by taking the time to capitalize on the variables that are available to all bladesmiths everywhere: steel selection, time, temperature, thermal cycles and the desire to experiment.

Epilogue: 52100 From A Metallurgist's View

The previous discussions concerning forging and heat treating methods that, in my opinion, lead the way to truly high performance blades, were written to lead the way to the discussion, "52100 From A Metallurgists View." There is more to the story.

Much has been said about sophisticated machine shops and complex heat treating methods that require equipment far beyond the means of the average knifemaker. How far can an individual go in a one-man shop with limited funds available, in the search for a truly high performance blade? I believe that as in all ventures of man, our greatest obstacles are those of our individual imagination and prejudice.

Rick Dunkerley, American Bladesmith Society Master Smith, has dedicated his bladesmithing abilities to the search for truly high performance blades. Rich has visited my shop on several occasions and participated in marathon around the clock experimental sessions with me. It takes a special kind of desire to cram hundreds of sleepless hours of labor into less than a week. Rick has that kind of vision and devotion.

In 1996 at Wayne Goddard's open house following the Oregon Custom Knife Show, Rick publicly tested one of his 52100E blades forged from a one-inch-round bar of stock, against a steel that in my opinion may very well be one of the best steels currently available to the stock removal knifemaker. Repeated cutting tests were performed, followed by flex tests. Rick's blade cut within 10% of the performance level of a 440V test blade, then Rick preceded to flex his blade a full 180°,6 and 1/2 times before the edge cracked.

Phil Wilson, custom knifemaker, and one of the participants in the testing session, suggested that Rick submit the test blade to a metallurgist for thorough evaluation. He sug-gested Sam DiGiallonardo of Metallographic Laboratory Service..

In typical bladesmith fashion, Rick called them and worked out a trade, one of his knives for the analysis. Rick sent his test blade from the open house to the laboratory and soon received a call from the metallurgist wanting to know what kind of steel he was working with. He stated that he had never seen a grain structure in steel as fine as he found in the test blade. Rick assured him that the steel started as 52100E. The metallurgist then preceded with the analysis. The results were discussed in the article.

In this incidence, results were obtained by an intricate combination of the right steel, proper forging and thermal cycles. The blade materials, which are tough, abrasion resistant, hard and strong, were put together in one blade, by a blade-smith dedicated to the high performance knife. His methods and equipment were those readily to the bladesmith without the highly sophisticated equipment some may feel is neces-sary. Dedication to the development of the high performance blade is the prime prerequisite. Our frontiers are only limited by our imagination and fortitude to explore. Thanks to Rick Dunkerley, we now know that the high potential of the forged blade, is no longer theory, just facts.

I strongly believe that the results of the metallurgists analysis indicate a milestone in the development of the forged blade. This was not accomplished in one stroke of the ham-mer, but was the result of thousands of hours of hard work. Those who contributed heavily to this success are many. Rick Dunkerley, Barry Gallagher, Wayne Goddard, Dick Iiams, John Strohecker and all who supported our search played a roll in our success; no one man could have done it alone.

The Quest for Excalibur

In testing his blades over the past ten years, the author said he's cut over 150 feet of 1-1/8-inch rope into 1/32-inch pieces.

In the past five issues of Blade, I've presented a discussion concerning my methods of forging knives. I don't claim there's only one way to skin a cat or forge a blade. Any blade-smith who desires to push his blades to the upper limits of performance can do so, providing he develops a comprehensive testing program designed to specifically evaluate the qualities of his knives in reference to the job for which they are intended. Testing, critical evaluation, unlimited curiosity, honest elbow grease, imagination and dedication are the prerequisites for a high-performance knife. I've found no short-cuts.

The methods discussed have stood the test of time and are what works for me in my shop with the steel I use, and are only a portion of the total process employed to develop my knives. My statements are not meant to condemn any other makers' practices. I didn't intend to offend any individuals, institutions or groups in the world of knives.

Years ago I experimented with various combinations of steels in the hopes of developing a truly high-performance Damascus blade. I tried numerous combinations and even added some alloys to the mix in the form of welding and brazing materials. After numerous failures I came up with a layered, angel-hair Damascus piece that out cut any blade I'd ever tested by a wide margin.

My first inclination was to make a large number of blades using the "new formula." Fortunately, calving time and spring farm work kept me too busy and the new "improved" blade waited on the bench through the cold months into spring. That spring, fellow Blade field editor Wayne Goddard was coming to my shop to share time about knives and I enthusiastically waited to demonstrate my "improved" Damascus.

Wayne arrived and I casually handed him the blade and asked him to cut some rope with it. I anxiously watched, expecting his awe after cutting with what I thought was the greatest knife ever. Wayne made three cuts on a piece of rope and the blade quit cutting! He looked at me like I was working some kind of joke on him. I figured that the knife just needed sharpening and would then prove itself in the next cutting test as the best Damascus ever made.

Wayne sharpened the blade and it again quit after three cuts. I took the blade, sharpened it and once more went back to the cutting board. Again, only three cuts and it was as dead as my old silver-plated butter knife. Wayne stood there waiting for the punch line, and all I could do was stutter around about how great the blade had performed six months ago! Evidently, the alloys I added to the mix of steels had the effect of producing an outstanding knife with a very short life span. Probably the alloys had softened the blade over time, along with variations in temperature.

From this incident I learned a very important lesson that has stuck with me ever since. Never consider any event in the development of a high-performance knife a success until it has proved itself over a period of time, experiencing as many realistic variables that it will face in actual use, such as physical force, temperature, moisture and other aspects of the environment in which the knife will work.

The Quest

Most of my past 25 years have either been shared with cows or making knives. Many a knife has hung on my belt in that time. Some didn't last very long; others did their job for years. I can't count the number of animals I've field dressed and the other tasks my experimental knives have undertaken. I do know that in the past 10 years I've cut over 150 feet of 1 1/8-inch hemp rope into 1/32-inch pieces, destroyed more knives than most men own in a lifetime, and invested thousands of hours seeking the best blade I can make.

The material that I write about in Blade is based on time-tested methods, materials and designs that work for me in my shop and in the environment in which I live. I don't claim that they're the only ways to make a knife, or that they'll appeal to everyone, nor are my methods set in stone. I continue to learn more every day.

I write about the lessons I've experienced over time for several reason's. First, if they can be of benefit to the world of knives, I don't want them to die with me. Second, I hope to help keep the search for the best blade man will ever know active in the minds of all who wish to join in the quest.

The world of knives consists of men, and tradition is the foundation on which mankind maintains stability. There are many excellent knifemakers and collectors who devote their talents to the preservation of the traditional blades of the past.

If this is where lies their Excaliber, I feel it both fitting and proper that they continue their edge quest.

When I first forged knives with experienced bladesmiths who graciously shared their knowledge concerning the basics of forging, I thought I knew all there was to know. Now, after years of forging, I have many more questions than answers.

I strongly feel the sun is just rising on the day of the forged blade. How that blade will appear when the sun sets will depend on the dreams and dedication of all future smiths who pursue the frontiers of the unknown in order to make the best blade they can.

I don't write about knives to aggravate other makers or intentionally step on any toes. To those who were personally offended by my writing, I apologize. If, by my discussions, curiosity is aroused and new frontiers are explored, I'll consider myself a success. The forged blade is based on an infinite number of variables. No single man could ever have enough time to consider all of them. Any bladesmith who claims to know them all only fools himself. Should my invitation to explore new territory challenge others to action, their contributions will be welcome. There's plenty of room for everybody.

The King Tut dagger brought to many individuals visions of an Excaliber of Tut's time. The dagger served Tut well in that his legend lives on in the hearts of men in the world of knives who may fail to remember him for whatever else it was that he accomplished. My personal Excaliber is the development of a knife that would be the most prized possession of any man of any time, past, present, or future, who lives with nature and needs a friend on whom he can count. The thought that my conclusions may be less than perfect does not escape me, nor will the fear of error silence me. All I can say is that the information I write is based on the trails I've followed and is presented honestly in the interest of nurturing the ultimate functional forged blade of the future.

CHAPTER 4

Dr. Lucie knife in the purest Scagel fashion. (Lucie photo)

Legends

The history of the knife is repeated each time a new knifemaker makes his first knife. As he makes that knife, and the ones that follow, he will share many of the thoughts of those who came before him. Stone Age man made knives to survive, as modern man does today. To many, making knives is just a job, and when looking at their work it is glaringly apparent.

There are, however, knifemakers who make knives because they want to. They are driven by the desire to make a knife their way, coming from their hand, lead by dreams of achieving the best knife ever made. This quest leads to better and better knives, and dreamers see visions of perfection. Dreams lead us to the world of knives; dreams keep us there and open a path to the future.

Seduced by the Iron Mistress

Editor's note: Following is the author's imaginative way of explaining what his "dream" Bowie knife-or "The Iron Mistress" - is, and how it has inspired his knifemaking. To expand on his theme, he asked some of his fellow makers to submit the knives they've made that were inspired by the Iron Mistress ideal. Those knives are shown herein.

The author forged his Iron Mistress from 52100 steel. The guard is brass, the handle is sheep horn.

The summer's work was done. The nights were getting shorter and it was a perfect evening. Laying next to the Wind River, I could feel the comfort that men have felt at this time of year for thousands of years. The leaves were just beginning their fall spectacle of color and a mule deer was working a little polish on his new set of antler. Within the next few hours the sound of his splash would break the tranquil sound of the river while he crossed to the hay field on the other side.

My three Labradors laid with me. A piece of cottonwood made a pillow that was good enough. As I drifted in and out of light sleep, my thoughts shifted from the day's events to the dreams of more. Watching the water in its endless progression to the timeless sea, I felt at one with all time, knowing that all water is connected. Water has witnessed and cleansed and carried man throughout his time. I could see Cleopatra's majestic ships of Egypt, the Bismarck sinking to its resting place, the cannons of the Monitor and the CSS Virginia belching their black smoke and fire, and more.

I remembered the movie *The Iron Mistress*, and the scene when Alan Ladd as the legendary James Bowie threw the blade world's better-known Iron Mistress" into the water to her final resting place. As always I mourned her loss. I was just a kid when I saw the movie. I dreamed of the Iron Mistress laying in the murky depths of that river for years. I fan-

tasized that one day I would be the one to rescue her, and together we would be champions.

A full moon rose over the cottonwoods across the water and spilled a new set of shadows for us to feel. Then my thoughts centered upon a calm in the midst of the flowing water. Surrounded by the ripples of the river, the calm seemed to stand still with an intensity that demanded my full attention. Then from the depths of the water I could see the light that only comes from within. Slowly an object arose from the depths, exploding from the surface with a calm beauty that caressed my heart.

There she was, the greatest lady of all time, the lady of legend-the Iron Mistress. We were alone. She was beautiful; her lines, her scent, her touch were all beyond my ability to describe. Her essence totally surrounded me. I wanted to touch her. She accepted my warmth and we shared our thoughts.

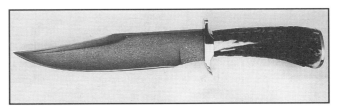

(Above) Once called the Wizard of Wootz by this magazine, it fits that Al Pendray would make his Iron Mistress with a wootz blade.

I inquired as to her birth. She remembered and without hesitation told me of the creative potential provided by the fire, and how the loving blows of the hammer matched with the guiding force of the anvil shaped her essence. She spoke of how the knowledge and skills of thousands of years and many craftsmen and soldiers came together in two men, the bladesmith and the warrior. She spoke of how the knowledge, care and imagination of two men merged to build within her more than could ever be seen by those without faith. Evil would scoff at her power and, when defeated, would become even more obsessed with destroying her. She could not be defeated. She would lose some battles but never be defeated.

She knew that hers would be a short life (though she could have lived forever in some museum or private collection), but that she would always be in the hearts of men who see and feel more than what is needed for mere survival. It was her fight during life that granted her a place of honor in some man's heart.

We spoke of the lonely lives that men of honor may be forced to live; how her memory and what she stood for could,

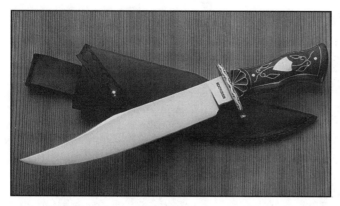

Of his Iron Mistress, Jay Hendrickson writes: "Although I prefer to think that the clip-styled Bowie would be closer to my personal design of an Iron Mistress, my imagination quickly can visualize a blade with a spear or even a trailing point. I guess what I am trying to say is that the Iron Mistress just can't be a one-styled knife."(Weyer Photo)

Robbin Hudson's Iron Mistress has a five-bar composite Damascus blade with his trademark - the flame edge. (Editor's note: Hudson is recovering from serious injuries suffered ion a recent car wreck. "The Blade" wishes him well.

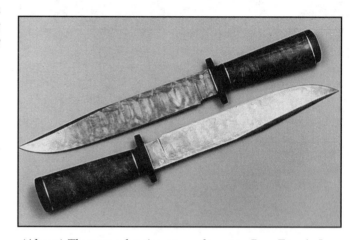

(Above) These two bowies come closest to Don Fogg's Iron Mistress, though he said that if he had a choice beyond a knife he'd probably select an axe or a sword.

make their fight a little better; how her power could bring light to those battles to be fought in darkness; and that those who would know of her could find hope possible where none existed. Many times there is more to loneliness than just being alone.

Together we were totally content. No care or stress could enter our domain. She encouraged me to enjoy the things that made her what she was: her strength, her gently rounded sides, her strong back, her handle as smooth as velvet. Her cutting edge was keen and sharp. There were no extras. Everything was perfect. There was nothing to distract from her pure beauty, nothing to hide, nothing to distort-she was what she was, and she was the best.

We spoke of battles past and those of the future. Men who stand upon principles and fight to make the world a little better need an ally to stand with them, someone they can count on if only to cut the sting of loneliness. She would always be there, never to abandon the champions of justice. She would never judge their cause, only stand by her men in their time of valor.

We talked of her sisters, the Iron Mistresses of past times and places and peoples long gone, many of them never recorded in history, their names and faces lost forever. Her great-grandmother was made of copper; before her came ancestors made from wood and bone and stone. We spoke of the battles, great and small, though in even the greatest battle each and every warrior stood alone, as alone as all men facing survival or death, from stone age man facing starvation, building his shelter and securing his food with his "stone mistress," to the explorer of space thousands of years later.

Whenever all was at stake, she was there. She kissed men goodbye when the battle was lost and sent them on their way,

their last earthly memory being her caress to their hand as life's warmth cooled. She held my hand and all I could feel was her essence. She fit my hand perfectly, nothing sharp, nothing cold or rough, just her power, her warmth, her companionship. What more could a man want?

We spoke of her faraway sisters, the tanto, the dagger and the machete. Man can find her wherever he is, in the jungles, discount stores-even on Park Avenue. She is everywhere waiting for her man to find her and take her to his side to do battle in the rain forests and deserts, mountains and oceans and skies. She presides everywhere man is, from the boardrooms and courts and city streets to the shelter of his home. She exists to stand by her man. She is what you see, she is what you touch, she is what you feel, she is what you dream, and a whole lot more.

The sun's warmth brought in a new day. The Iron Mistress had left my hand but her memory filled me with peace.

Joseph Szaski forged this "lady" out of D2. The blade is 9 inches long and the handle is Micarda. His address: 29 Carrol, Dept. BL, Wappingers Falls, NY 12590 (914) 297-5397.

The night had been one of wonder and contentment; the opportunity to be with one so great left me grateful and content. Even though I can no longer touch her, her memory is and will always - be with me.

Addresses For Makers In The Story

Don Fogg, Dept. BL, Rt. 6, Box 107, Jasper, AL 35501-8813 (205) 483-0822

Ed Fowler, Dept. BL, Willow Bow Ranch, POB 1519, Riverton, WY 82501 (307) 856-9815

Jay Hendrickson, Dept. BL, 4204 Ballenger Creek, Frederick, MD 21701 (301) 663-6923

Gil Hibben, POB 13, Dept. BL, LaGrange, KY 40031 (502) 222-1397

Robbin Hudson, Dept. BL, 22280 Frazier, Rock Hall, MD 21661 (410) 639-7273

Al Pendray, Dept. BL, Rt. 2, Box 1950, Williston, FL 32696 (904) 528-6124

Antique Bowies—
Blades & Brothers Against One Another

Bruce Voyles made the audience "smell the smoke and hear the cannon roar."

Blades used by brother against brother in what symposium moderator Bill Adams would call "the late unpleasantness" were the focus of the 4th Annual Bowie Symposium May 16, 1996, at the Waverly Hotel in Atlanta.

Organized by James Batson and held the day before the 15th Annual Blade Show & International Cutlery Fair, the symposium outlined the romance of Civil War bowies, among other topics. For example, in a presentation entitled, "Bowies On The Battlefield," Bruce Voyles characterized a confederate bowie as a "symbol of defiance." On the other hand, a federal bowie was described as a "badge of marshal intent" by bowie aficionado Allen Richards.

Symposium contributors also included Logan Sewell, James Corry, Floyd Ritter, Norm Flayderman and Levon Register. Their well-researched presentations provided valuable bowie information that would have taken years of research to discover on your own.

Logan Sewall and other participants provided many fine Bowies for our inspecion. The fine examples of history and craftsmanship were discussed by interested students of the Bowie, each seeing that which his past experience brought to his vision. While one described gold and silver fittings of a handle and sheath, Wayne Goddard noticed that the rivet holes in the tang of an old forged blade were the result of a hot punch rather than drilled with a drill press. The many separate messages sent by past craftsmen to the past, present and future, each received by an individual eye, hearing the individual message sent and more.

In "Georgia Bowie Knives," Adams described an unusual bowie he referred to as "a lasso knife," so named because it was believed to have been designed as a throwing piece. It had a ring at the base of the handle to which a rope could be tied to retrieve the bowie after it had been thrown. Adams said the pieces probably never were used in battle and were more likely worn about the neck in camp. Another unusual bowie Adams highlighted was a double D-guard model, one with two D-guards on one handle!

Additional topics included Register's "Civil War Photos of Bowies," "Marcellus Cassius Clay" by Corry and Sewell's "Mississippi Bowie Knives." A descendant of Samuel Wells, one of the participants on James Bowie's side in the famous Sandbar Fight of 1827, Sewell's bowie pedigree is impeccable.

The symposium was concluded by the "Civil War Bowie Knife Show and Roundtable," in which the bowie authorities fielded questions and offered many rare antique pieces for audience inspection.

For more information on the symposium and future such events, contact Jim Batson, Dept. BL, 176 Brentwood, Madison, AL 35758 (205) 971-6860.

Mystery of the D-Guard Bowie

The author's D-guard bowie weights 3 lbs. and is 26 inches long overall.

The annual Riverton Memorial Day Weekend Gun, Coin & Antique Show, coupled with the Wind River Muzzleloaders Blackpowder Shoot, has always been one of my favorite times of year. Contestants at the shoot come from as far away as Europe to compete and enjoy the comradeship of others who share the love of a bygone era. Dealers, traders, contestants and enthusiasts from far and wide buy and sell guns, coins, antiques, leather gear and knives from, and representative of, the frontier days.

Each year the number of different knives on display and for sale seems to increase. Unlike the big knife shows, there aren't thousands of blades present, but there are enough to keep me talking knives most of the weekend. I've found several of my favorite antique blades at these events.

Laying on a dark corner of a table, partially covered with leather gear, I saw what appeared to be the handle of a D-Guard bowie. At first I thought it was a poorly made copy that started its antique career as a broken or worn-out machete or sword reworked to look like something special. Then, through the dust and dim light of the back room, I felt something special calling to me. I asked to look the bowie over and the dealer-who obviously lives in and loves the world of knives as many of us do-smiled and handed her to me. Meanwhile, he asked to look at the blade I was carrying. From that moment we were friends.

The more I examined the bowie, the more I became fascinated with the story she had to tell. The blade, covered with rust, is obviously forged. Her balance is as nice as they come and she is well preserved, though she has been in a wreck or two. The tip is bent, not broken. A crack in the cutting edge about 1 1/2 inches from the tip stops about halfway from the spine. Probably the tip of the blade had been bent, then straightened without breaking, though the cutting edge had cracked. The edge is obviously hard but not too hard, while the spine is soft and tough. The scars indicate that the man who hardened and tempered her knew what he was doing and had produced a trustworthy knife.

As I ran my fingers along the blade, I felt a nicely constructed convex shape flowing gracefully from the spine to the edge. The taper from the guard to the tip is excellent. The spine is comfortably rounded and the unsharpened false edge is uniform and capably done, flowing majestically from the rounded spine about 9 inches from the tip.

Through the rust and age she speaks of the devotion of her maker, the quality of his workmanship and his knowledge of cutting efficiency. The wood handle, surrounded by the D-Guard, is capped with tapered, seamless, forged-steel ferrules that ensure a long, functional life of the wood. Even if the handle should crack, it would not come off the knife. The handle and the forged ferrules are egg shaped and fit my hand comfortably. Though the handle has aged many years, it is still tight and functional. Spiral grooves flow the length of the wood, providing a secure grip.

The D-Guard fits tight to the blade. The tang comes through the handle butt and the D-Guard, and is peened over to secure the handle and guard to the blade permanently. The knife weighs 3 lbs. The blade is 20 1/4 inches long. Overall, the knife is 26 inches long. The blade is 1 3/8 inches at its widest and 3/8-inch thick at the guard. There are no marks to identify the maker or the original owner.

The knife consists of simple materials, steel and properly harvested and cured wood. Still, she speaks of quality that easily transcends knives made from all the fancy materials

The cracked cutting edge indicates that the blade was differentially hardened (soft back, hard edge).

available to today's bladesmith. I inquired as to her price and her owner quoted a figure that was more than reasonable.

The Bowie Symposium

Ten days earlier, I had attended Jim Batson's 4th Annual Bowie Symposium conducted before the Blade Show & International Cutlery Fair. At the symposium, Bruce Voyles presented some interesting information on Confederate bowies.

According to Voyles, in 1862 the governor of Georgia contracted 17 different blacksmiths to provide the Confederacy with 4,000 Dguard bowies. The knives were to weigh 3 lbs. and cost $4.60 each. According to available records, 4,100 of the knives were made. With 17 different blacksmiths making the same knife, along with the likelihood that the smiths probably subcontracted another unknown number of smiths to help fill the order, there are undoubtedly a great many variations of the Georgia contract D-guard bowies. The thought struck me: Is the bowie I bought in Riverton an original Georgia D-guard bowie, or was it made in another time and place for another war or individual?

To find out as much as I could about the knife, I discussed her with three knowledgeable devotees to blades and the knives of the Confederacy: Batson, one of the world's best bowie researchers and an ABS master smith; Wayne Goddard, also an ABS master smith and an expert at smoking out a knife's heritage; and Voyles, former owner and publisher of *The Blade Magazine*, and a son and student of the Confederacy.

In Search Of A Pedigree

Voyles said the drop at the butt of the hilt is a "dead giveaway" that she was probably made in the Philippines sometime before World War II." He added that she was not made as a replica of the Confederate D-guard bowies, but that she

is a genuine artifact of the time and place where she was made. If she was made in the Philippines, she is not of the usual Filipino kind I've seen, but made by one of the island's best knifemakers.

Batson said the steel looks like shear steel, which indicates that the knife probably was made prior to 1900. He advised that the country of origin might be determined by the kind of wood in the handle, as most of the original Confederate Dguard bowies were handled with oak or Southern hardwood, and most pieces of this type had handles of wood from the area where they were made. At this time, I don't know what kind of wood is in the handle.

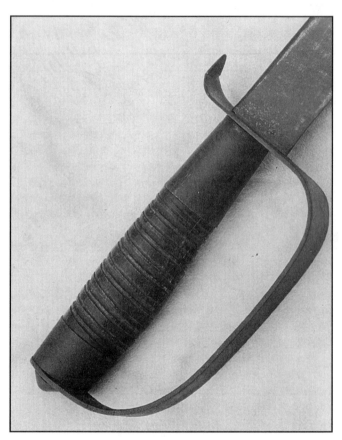

Note the spiral grooves in the handle and the tapered ferrules that secure the handle to the blade.

Batson indicated that the methods used in the knife's construction as indicated by the ferrules are the fully developed techniques of a bladesmith who knew what he was doing in the early years of the forged blade. He added that the blade was finished with a file and stones.

Goddard said, "I'm not smart enough to tell if it's an original Confederate bowie, but there are many things that point to it having been made in the 1800s," such as:

1) The type of construction in the handle with the iron bolsters or collars;

2) The blade appears to have been forged of steel made by forge welding smaller pieces together. Either that or what is known as cementite or the "steeling" process, where iron was folded and welded multiple times in a charcoal fire to add carbon to the blade;

3) The blade finish appears to have been done with files and hand stones;

4) The oxidation on the guard makes the guard material look like real wrought iron. The cracked area in the guard makes it look like wrought iron that is "hot short" (Editor's note: hot short refers to wrought iron that is forged at too low a temperature, which can cause cracking);

5) The cracked portion of the blade indicates that the blade was selectively hardened or tempered, not usually something a counterfeiter would do;

6) It is the right length and weight for a D-guard bowie; and

7) The distal and wedge tapers are "right on."

SOLVED: The D-Guard Bowie Mystery

There are faint similarities between the author's Flipino D-guard piece (inset) and this old, unmarked Confederate bowie. (the latter is from The Antique Bowie Knife Book*)*

The story on the D-guard bowie ("Mystery Of The D-Guard Bowie," November '96 Blade) inspired some interesting feedback. At the California Custom Knife Show and in my shop the knife has been visited by bladesmiths, collectors and students of historical blades. Phone calls and letters have brought fairly consistent information concerning her heritage.

For the most part, bladesmiths who've inspected her have been very interested in her design and appreciative of the workmanship that went into her construction. Some traced her lines with the intention of making one of their own. She has been appreciated by all makers who've visited her as an example of top-quality work by a bladesmith whose dedication to his craft continues to speak of excellence long beyond his time.

Dave Kliner, a devoted collector and student of antique edged pieces, sent me photos of authentic Confederate Dguard bowies and convincingly excludes her from the ranks of the arms of the Confederacy. Several other knowledgeable students of the forged blades of the era voiced the same opinion.

Several students of Filipino bladesmithing examined the bowie and said she was a typical example of one of the unnamed higher-echelon bladesmiths of that part of the world. Judging from her physical attributes, they said she probably was made sometime during the mid-to-late 1880s.

Through the years I've seen the blades of Filipino blade-smiths and have felt that their art was somewhat second rate when compared to that of bladesmiths from other areas. It never occurred to me that the knives that I was seeing were mostly hastily made souvenirs sold to soldiers and tourists during and after World War 11, and were not representative of the Philippines' best workmanship.

This blade and the knife enthusiasts who've taken the time to share information about her have provided me with a new appreciation for the excellence and dedication of the early Filipino bladesmiths.

These knives are not commanding high-dollar prices in the American market when compared, for example, to authentic Confederate D-guard bowies. However, these Filipino blades are an excellent model of superior workmanship and are well worth the money.

Epilogue:

The D-Guard Bowie - Since the two articles on the D-Guard Bowie, many more hands have held her at knife shows. one of the top living authorities on Bowies firmly proclaimed her to be a true Confederate D-Guard Bowie of high quality. While another of wide renown claimed her heritage to be Phillipene. To me the message is clear, no aged knife without a clear and absolutely indisputable heritage must depend upon the eye of the present to judge her true nature. Many opinions will honestly contradict each other. When you see a knife that you like, do not depend upon her lineage to determine her value, counterfeits can be all the original pretended to be and more. We are best to judge a knife for the quality of workmanship and design we can appreciate and place her value in accord to our taste. As she traveled with us to various knife shows her value ranged from hundreds to thousands of dollars. She was not and is not for sale, I appreciate her for what she is, an absolute tribute to quality workmanship of the past. It matters not where she comes from in history, she was born by the hand of a master and that is all that matters to me. Her place is in our home and we get along well together.

CHAPTER 5

(Gallagher photo)

Interactions
with the Outside World

No one stands alone. China tried by building a great wall to keep the rest of the world out. While it worked for a time. the isolation ended up costing them more than it was worth. A knifemaker has to interact with the outside world, or he will be so far behind, he won't know the difference. The following are some thoughts on how to make the interactions more palatable.

8 Keys For Modern Knifemakers

You should entertain any question about knives - not just your own - and knifemaking in general. Here Jay Hendrickson explains forging to interested onlookers at the ABS forging demonstration during the 1995 Blade Show.

Getting started in knifemaking is like getting started in any business. There are a lot of ways to do it. Most of them work, some are better than others, and there are some real wrecks waiting to happen. However, there's one thing you should always remember: Success or failure can depend on factors that don't concern the quality of your knives. Your customers must be able to rely on you, and all they have to build that trust is your reputation.

Your reputation as a knifemaker is built one step at a time. Over a lifetime of hard work, study, creativity and ethical practices, you can climb as high as you want. One slip and it can be a long way down. Following are eight areas that can give a maker trouble and how you should handle them.

1) Deposits

Some successful and reputable makers take deposits and have experienced no difficulties. This discussion does not reflect on them.

When working as a lawyer, Abraham Lincoln declined to charge or accept large retainers on cases because he said it reduced his motivation to work the case. For a man like Lincoln to experience motivational problems when paid in advance is something makers should consider in their business practices.

Accepting a deposit for a knife can be a trap. It's simple to accept cash in advance with good intentions of fulfilling an obligation. But what if you then experience some "wrecks" that set you behind financially? The next thing you know, you've spent the money you took for a deposit. You have bills to pay, customers wanting knives with cash in hand, you like

to eat, and the man who paid in advance waits and waits. He calls wanting his knife and you have to stall, and pretty soon you've made an enemy out of a friend.

Sometimes a customer orders a knife so unique that if he doesn't buy it, you'll have a hard time selling it to someone else. It may be that he wants his name engraved on it or it may be a design that no one else would want. In such cases I usually suggest some kind of pay-as-the-work-progresses agreement. Talk it over carefully with the customer and make sure that you both understand the agreement.

2) Delivery Dates

As the demand for your knives increases, you'll have to develop a waiting list. Waiting lists are tough to handle. I'd much rather talk to the customer and have the knife in the mail the next day. Unfortunately, that isn't possible. All you can do is be honest. There are too many complications in my life for me to guarantee a specific delivery date. I promise to have a knife ready as soon as I can, estimate an approximate delivery date, and do my best to meet the deadline. Customers usually receive delivery in the order that they were placed on the waiting list.

A suggestion for knife customers who have been on a waiting list and haven't heard from the maker for some time: Don't be bashful about calling or writing to let the maker know you are still interested. One maker, who I won't name, lost all records of his waiting list when his house burned. He knew that there were a lot of people wanting his knives, but he didn't have any names, addresses or phone numbers to get back to them.

3) Correspondence

Years ago when I was getting started making knives, I wrote letters to some makers whom I respected. I identified myself as a maker and asked questions about getting started. The best of the makers responded within a few days. Some of them never answered. D' Holder wrote a great letter that I still have. He had more than enough to do to excuse him from writing a new guy tapping him for information.

The lesson was simple: Whenever correspondence comes to me about knives, I answer it within a few days if at all possible. My wife reads the letter, and I dictate the answers. Usually the return letter is in the mail in a few days.

4) Employees

You'll do a lot better making knives if you've got good help. If you have to hire them, do it. Be cautious about letting anyone represent you who doesn't share your ideals. Your reputation depends on all who work with you. A grumpy employee can hurt what you're trying to build without your knowing it.

5) Self Control

One of my first knife shows was in a big city where I didn't know any makers. I was set up next to a maker who was pretty well known. His knives were the fancy kind and not intended to see much use. One well-dressed man was walking through the show with his son. He asked a man in Western dress who looked like he might know what a using blade was all about to recommend a camping knife for him to buy for his son. The newly appointed "knife expert" approached my neighbor's table and picked out a crossbred fantasy knife, claiming that it was the best using knife in the place.

The maker looked at me and smiled as he put the money in his billfold. We knew that the toughest thing the so-called knife expert had ever skinned probably came from the vegetable area of the grocery store. The last time his boots were near a horse was probably when they were still hide on the beef the horse was following in the feed lot.

Having been promoted to a knife authority, the "expert" started making himself obvious. Eventually, he walked over to my table and looked over my knives. He picked one up, looked at it like it was something bad, and slammed it back down on the table, bouncing it off another of my knives. It made enough noise to cause folks in the area to look, as well as damaging my knives. My first inclination was to help him outside where we could talk about the consequences of his being a jerk.

There was a time in my life when I rarely remembered my grandfather's words about controlling my temper. Had this been one of those times, I would probably be remembered as the maker who got in a fight at the show in 1982. That kind of reputation is real easy to follow a guy around. It wasn't that the "expert" didn't deserve some sound discipline or that I wasn't willing to do it. It was just that I bit the bullet and made my grandfather proud.

Whenever in the knife community, whether at a show or on the phone talking knives, you are building an image that will follow you and your knives forever. Don't ever say or do anything you don't want on the cover of Blade magazine. There are a lot of little things that can irritate you, but if you remember they are little things, they will stay that way.

6) Professionalism

Should a customer ask you about another maker's knives, discuss the good points of the knives and keep the negative thoughts to yourself. Speaking ill of other makers only serves to create animosity in a world in which we all want to be. While controversy, discussion and debate make for better knives, there is no room for dishonesty, jealousy and hate. The less we let it in, the more content we all will be.

7) Customer Relations

There are some folks who come to shows and makers' shops who are poor communicators. It may have been a stroke or accident that left them that way, but they mean well. Makers aren't at shows only to sell knives; they are at shows to introduce others to themselves and to promote the world of knives.

One time years ago I was looking at a knife that a young man had made. It had a coat-hanger handle and a sheath fashioned from copper pipe. To him it was the best knife ever. To me it showed a lot of creativity, devotion and hard work.

While the boy and I discussed his knife, a big spender walked up. He waited for a second and then walked away. He didn't make it back to my table at that show. However, I would not trade the time spent with the young boy for all the cash the big spender had in his pocket. The memory still enriches me; the cash would have been spent long ago.

8) Handling Criticism

While compliments make you feel good, seek critics who are knowledgeable and willing to criticize the knives you make. Listen carefully with an open mind whenever any customer has a complaint about your knives. If you've made a bad knife, you want to know it and should be eternally grateful to the man who was honest and considerate enough to bring his complaint to you. Everyone makes mistakes; that's human nature. The ones who make those mistakes are the ones who need to know it. That's part of the road to better knives. Encourage criticism, use it to your advantage, and keep making knives. Some complaints come from a lack of understanding. When that happens, you didn't cover enough ground with the customer when you sold the knife.

The last thing you want is a dissatisfied customer telling everyone what's wrong with your knives. Even if he is a total jerk, usually you're better off apologizing profusely for your error, giving him his money back, smiling and shaking his

The author (left) stresses the importance of working with people who share your ideals the way apprentice John Strohecker (right) does.

hand, and thanking him for the valuable service he has done you. It's okay to quietly walk up to your room and slug the wall a few times just as long as he doesn't know it.

Epilogue:

I always try to keep time about knives good times for all. I am not always successful. While talking knives at a knife show I was engaged by another knifemaker in an extensive discussion about multiple quench techniques and results. We were worlds apart and there was no compromise. As time passed, the words got louder, bystanders became more and I could feel my blood pressure rise. I tried to terminate the discussion, but he persisted. Suddenly he gave me an odd look and left, I could not understand why but was grateful. Later I heard that he told another knifemaker that I "growled at him'".

I train dogs on a daily basis. I learned the most effective dog discipline from my Black Labrador Blue. When she needed to get tough with one of her pups, she simply rolled it over on its back and growled at it. Many times when severe measures are necessary in order to get one of my dogs attention I do as she did, roll them over on their back, bare my teeth and growl at them. This is a very impressive method of discipline,that works and never physically hurts the dog. Evidently I had from habit, without meaning to, used the same technique on him. He has never engaged me in conversation since that time.

Etiquette:
Pass The Billets, Please!

(Above) Knifemaker Ed Fowler says he loves sharing time with people who like knives but cautions that you be sure to call to line up a visit - and then call the day before the visit to remind him.

Blade Editor's note.- Last issue - "The Blade Magazine" presented "Time Share," a story about how several knifemakers have worked and learned together. In the following story, the author offers a few tips on how to behave — whether you're just curious or there to learn how to make knives - when visiting a maker's shop.

Many knifemakers welcome visitors to their shops. All makers like to take breaks, and sharing time with people who like knives is what knifemaking is all about. However, just because makers are self employed doesn't mean that they always have unlimited time to spend at activities other than knifemaking. They have to make a living and all they have to sell is their time spent making knives.

Sometimes the maker's time gets a little short, especially before a knife Show. Call in advance if you want to visit and, when it comes to the more forgetful knifemakers like me, call again to remind them the day before your visit. Try to avoid arriving unannounced but if circumstances preclude planning, give the visit a try. Don't be offended if he doesn't have time for you; we all have bad days and you may just be catching him in the middle of a deadline.

A maker's shop is what you see—and a whole lot more. Some makers spend a lot of time experimenting, testing and making knives, and very little time cleaning up. Rest assured, my dogs and I like my shop the way it is. We are comfortable.

We know where things are and want them where they are. We spend two to three times as much time in the shop as we do in the house. The makers shop is his castle, bread and butter, and pride and joy. Don't try to change it on your first visit, you just may be walking all over the makers ego. I get a little aggravated when folks start handling what is mine without permission. There are reasons for this. Some are related to safety, some to economics. Leaving fingerprints on a polished blade at the wrong time can leave a lasting impression.

Many of us used to smoke. I stopped after my doctor told me that I had to quit smoking or quit making knives. I quit smoking. Grinding steel, bone, sheep horn and wood smells, but it is nothing like the aroma of a cigarette to the non-smoker, especially one who liked to smoke I suggest that you do as he does. If he smokes, go ahead and smoke with him. If he doesn't, try to stay downwind and your visit will go better.

Park your vehicle in an out-of-the-way place. If in doubt, ask the maker where he would like you to park. Also, if you have children with you, keep them under control. Knifemakers' shops are not usually designed with children in mind. Well-behaved kids are welcome anywhere. Kids who run wild are a hazard to their health and can wear your welcome out real fast.

Should others visit the shop while you are there, don't try to sell them knives or impress them with your knowledge and experience. Again, you are in another maker's world and all accolades are rightfully his. Visitors who have made themselves welcome forever in my shop are often those who bring food. One makers wife actually baled hay for me while her husband and I made knives. Other wives have cooked meats, cleaned house, mowed my lawn, brought mice for my rattlesnake, brushed my dog, Blue, and bottle-fed a calf. None of this was expected but it sure was nice.

If you are invited to another maker's shop to make knives, another set of rules applies. Always put every tool, piece of steel, pencil, ruler, rag, bottle and chair back in the exact place you got it. Be extra careful with his equipment. Some of it may be new, some of it may look like it arrived on the Mayflower. Nonetheless, it is his and it works for him in his shop.

Whenever you use any of a maker's tools or equipment, be prepared to replace or repair anything that breaks under your hand. What just broke may not be worth $10 at an auction, but replacing it could very well run several hundred dollars. The maker will have to replace it. You broke it, it's up to you to make it right. If you can't accept this responsibility, don't use his equipment.

When you look at a maker's shop, you see vast quantities of steel and handle materials. Large quantities may indicate

(Above) "Rest assured, my dogs and I like my shop the way it is...We know where things are and want them where they are...Don't try to change it on your first visit." - Ed Fowler

that the materials are cheap when actually you may be seeing the maker's major investment. He may have spent a lot of time finding the handle material and waited years to get it ready to go into a knife. Go easy if he doesn't offer to fill your

pick-up with whatever it is you like. He probably doesn't want to part with it.

Every time a sanding belt wears out, it costs money. In all probability the maker is not independently wealthy and has devoted a major part of his life building what you see in his shop, as well as his abilities. What you see may look like it cost a fortune. It is worth a fortune to him, also. It is best to pay your way if you can. Spending a few hours in a maker's shop can advance your knifemaking career by years. I paid for most of my knifemaking education. Two thousand dollars a week working with a knowledgeable craftsman is a cheap price if you are interested in becoming a top maker. Knowledge and ability can't be taken from you, you have to earn it. I spent years getting through the "first grade" as a maker. Investing a little time and money with the right maker is more than worth it.

Buffers are the most dangerous piece of equipment in many shops. They are also a valuable piece of equipment and tend to be temperamental. I dope my buffers with special compounds, some of them in a special way. Put the wrong compound on a buffer and I am going to spend a few hours getting it right. I don't know about other makers but in my shop it is best to let me tend the buffers.

Safety is a full-time job. Don't leave a bare sharpened blade sticking out of a vice. Don't pile stuff on the floor where the maker is used to walking. He may be used to stepping over the black Labradors but that black box is something else. When a maker is working on a knife and concentrating on one of the critical finishing touches, wait till he is through to ask questions. Talking when he's preoccupied will result in incomplete answers or a knife bouncing off the wall.

Mostly I have been talking from my experiences. Some thoughts from other makers are also included here. I haven't mentioned names simply to avoid hurting feelings. The rules are really pretty simple. Remember that you are a guest in another person's world. Treat him and his domain with respect and dignity and everything will work out best for all concerned.

The Revenuers

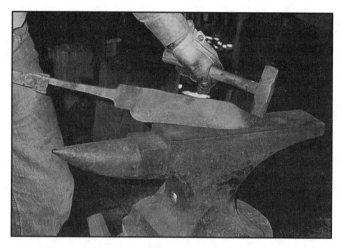

"Trying to explain anything to a revenuer is like talking to your anvil: It listens, but it won't do much." (Joe Keeslar photo)

Like most knifemakers, I started out making knives and giving them away. Sometimes it was hard to find someone to give a knife to, that is how I built up an inventory, just ran out of folks to give knives to. I started selling them. At first they sold pretty well, but there are only so many folks in Wyoming to buy custom knives. The whole state of Wyoming has less people a whole lot of big cities.

I set up at a "Christmas Fair" along with a whole lot of other folks that make things hoping that someone out there would want to buy them. My Daughter, Cindy, figured she should get into the act, so she made a bunch of suckers to sell. The first night of the fair there were a lot of people' came to see what they could pick up for Christmas. Most all of them bought a sucker from my daughter. I didn't sell a knife. Some folks stayed and talked knives while they was waiting to buy a sucker, but they was just being polite.

The second day she was pretty tuckered, after being up all night making suckers, she even doubled the price. That Saturday must have set the record for folks eating suckers, she sold out by 2:00 p.m. She was down to just a few left to sell when the Revenuer showed up. He was all dressed up and looked about as natural as high heels at a branding party. His hands was so clean and nice, looked like he just came out of the Sears Catalog. He was the first person to show any real interest in my knives, he talked about them, asked prices and was amazed that anyone would buy a knife for $100, (not that anyone had, they was just priced that way so he figured they was valuable). He bought a sucker from my daughter Cindy, then asked me if I had a State Sales Tax Number. I told him no, and waited for what was coming, figuring he was about to tell me. Sure enough, he was a state revenuer, and I was in vi-

olation cause I didn't have a State Sales Tax Number.

I asked him how many other folks at the fair had sales tax numbers, he said that was why he was there, because the state was losing money by not getting paid taxes on what sales that we were taking away from the retail stores. I had a little trouble fingering how I was taking sales from the big stores, especially since I hadn't sold anything, I was just trying to sell something, maybe a knife.

I asked him "how about the kid's suckers"? He said, "We are not interested in small stuff." Cindy put his 50 cents in her cash box, it was so full the lid wouldn't close, she had to empty it a couple of times that morning and was getting worried that someone was going to steal her money whenever she left to do what little girls do at craft fairs when they aren't selling suckers. Just because I hadn't sold anything she was even watching me over her shoulder. I asked her if I could borrow a couple of bucks for a hamburger and a coke and she made me to sign a note promising to pay her back.

Getting back to the revenuer, he left me a bunch of official looking papers and told me to fill them out and send them into the state. So that I could start making up for all the money the state was losing because of me. I watched him walk down the isle, talking to the other folks selling their wares. He sure had a nice suit, new shoes and they was even shined real pretty. Most of us selling was wearing shoes that hadn't seen a shine in years.

When they started closing down the craft fair, I real carefully put the papers he left me in the trash with all of the other papers he had left the other folks. Don't get me wrong, I am not against paying taxes, some of them are necessary and they keep bureaucrats from having to work for a living. I had a sales tax license one time for a gunsmithing license when I used to repair pistols. The trouble was that I had to file returns every three months and most of the time I didn't owe anything. Just did the paper work for nothing. Except one time I about went to jail for not sending in the form saying I didn't owe anything. The Revenue officer who was taking me in asked me why I even bothered with the license when I didn't pay enough taxes to make it worth the states time to fool with me. I agreed with him and haven't had a sales tax license since. It would be different if they would let you pay once a year, but they don't, and they won't, so neither do I.

Anyway - I kept on trying to sell knives and every now and then I would meet another revenuer giving me a bunch of papers to fill out. I kept throwing them away and pretty soon they was sending me letters. Then the letters came with all kinds of official frail, like 'CERTIFIED', 'RETURN RECEIPT REQUESTED' and the like. As always I just threw them away. I could have tried to work it out on the up and up, but one thing I have found out about bureaucrats, especially revenuers is that they are born, then after they are about five years old they don't ever learn anything new again. Trying to explain anything to one of them is like talking to your anvil, it will listen, but don't do much.

Then came the day that I got an official visit from one of the big guys from Casper. It was winter and I was working in my shop when I notice this fancy new car pulling up outside. I figured out who he was real quick when I saw the State License plates and how pretty he looked. You would think that when they was wanting to talk to a real working man they could at least send a working man out so they could talk the same language.

He parked his car and walked over to the shop, being real careful to avoid stepping in any cow pies that are usually laying around outside my shop. I let him in the shop, I was going to talk to him outside just to hurry things up, cause it was cold outside and his suit was more useful keeping him pretty than it was at keeping him warm. I thought about it and decided that I would try being nice to him.

He asked if I was Ed Fowler and I said yup. (Just then I, figured how I was going to work things out!) He told me that he was from the state and that they had been talking to me for a long time, that they had sent me letters and that they was done fooling with me! I was either going to start paying sales tax or I was going to jail. He was right forceful about it so I got real apologetic. I told him that I didn't mean to aggravate the government and that I was sorry. I told him that I never could figure out what it was all the letters was all about and that I didn't get many letters.

He softened up some and started telling me that sales tax didn't cost me anything, that I just got it from folks that bought from me and I in turn gave it to his outfit. I told him that I knew how important taxes were for roads and all and we were agreeing real well. He handed me a big piece of paper and I held it out at arms length and tried to read what it said. I held it for a while and asked him what it was the first two syllable word said. He read it to me then handed me back the piece of paper. I worked at it for awhile then asked him what the second two syllable word said?

He said "HERE LET ME READ IT TO YOU"

He read that piece of paper so fast there was smoke coming off of the paper when he finished.

He asked "Do you understand?"

I said "no", and went right back to the first line and the third two syllable word. He talked about that piece of paper for awhile then decided to give up with the forms and just try to get me to sign.

He said that all I had to do was "agree to collect 3 percent".

I asked him "Three what per-cent"?

He said "three per-cent of one".

I said " a cent is pretty small how can you take three of one?"

He said "NO three P-E-R C-E-N-T

I said again three what P-E-R C-E-N-T?"

He said "Three Cents out of one-hundred",

I said one hundred cents?

He said "YEA"!!

I asked "How many per-cents??

He just kind of stood there for a while staring at the wall, then smiled and started putting numbers on a piece of paper. He pulled out a little calculator and started showing me all kinds of stuff. I asked him how that thing worked? He said "It didn't matter how it worked, just that it did and it could tell percents".

I said "WOW"!

He pushed buttons for a while then asked me to try.

I pushed lots of numbers and he told me what was per cents.

I asked him, "Where the numbers went when they weren't on the picture screen"?

He took his calculator and put it back in his pocket and asked, "Does anybody in your family read"?

I said "Sure, but them is awful big words"!

I could see that he was getting nervous to get back home cause he kept looking at his watch and he had over 100 miles to drive before quitting time.

Knowing how bureaucrats hate to make commitments that involve extra work, I knew we were getting close to a. deal. I told him "I knew how we could get it all figured out real easy. Whenever I sold a knife I would write all the numbers down on my wall and when he came to town, he could put his little machine to work and tell me how many percents I owed and I would pay him"

He looked at me for a while and asked, "How many knives do you sell a year"?

Now that right there was the question I was waiting for him to ask all this time.

I told him that I usually sold "one or two a year".

He looked at me like he was kind of relieved and said that it would be more trouble than it was worth to fool around with no more sales than I made."

He said goodbye and tiptoed through the snow and cow pies between my shop and his fancy car. My favorite horse, Monk, was mouthing some snow off of the hind-end of his vehicle. He eyeballed Monk, then climbed in his fancy outfit and headed out the road. He never looked back or waved goodbye. I didn't figure he was planning on coming back. I was kind of glad that we got along so well, you can deal with a bureaucrat if you aren't too smart about it.

Hammered And Forged:
A Diary Of The Abs Bladesmith School

(Editor's note: Ed Fowler is a member of the American Bladesmith Society and a regular contributor to "The Blade Magazine. " Ed was assigned by "The Blade" to keep a running diary of his stay at the Texarkana College/American Bladesmith School in order to give "The Blade's" readers an insider's look at one of the most ambitious knifemaking schools in the world. For more information about the school contact the ABS, attn: Bill Moran, P.O. Box 68, Dept. BL, Braddock Heights, MD 21714.)

Knives of the finest bladesmithing class-all of them Damascus steel. At the top is a billet of Damascus steel ready to fold and forge weld. (Fowler photo)

When I heard that Bill Moran would be teaching the first Damascus steel class at the Texarkana College/American Bladesmith School, I called Bill and inquired about the subject matter he intended to cover. As always he made it sound interesting and I decided this would be an excellent opportunity to enhance my knifemaking abilities under the direction of one of the finest gentlemen in the knifemaking field.

I contacted James Powell, bladesmithing school director, at his Texarkana College office. He advised me that there was a vacancy in the class and I promptly sent my check and made plane reservations far enough in advance to take advantage of the discount rates. From the start Mr. Powell let me know that I was welcome, and advised me of the commuter airline, ground transportation and flat put out the welcome mat. I have attended many schools in my time and I have to give Powell and Bill Hughes, who also has been instrumental in

the school's creation, credit-the American Bladesmith School wins first place for hospitality hands down.

Sunday afternoon I drove to the Holiday Inn at Hope, Arkansas, in a van supplied by the college. I registered and drove around to my room. Looking into the window of one of the rooms I saw three gentlemen involved in a lively discussion. I knew they had to be knifemakers and, sure enough, they were coming to the same class. Funny how that works-knifemakers often know other knifemakers by sight. That evening we got together for dinner and talked knives.

School Facilities and Classes

Monday morning breakfast at the Holiday Inn: six students, one guest and Bill Moran sat at the same table and naturally talked knives. We then drove from Hope to Washington, Arkansas, site of the school. This was my first trip to the school and I was definitely impressed. The lecture room joins the shop via an alcove. When you walk into the classroom, you know you are in school-desks, blackboard, books, and pictures of past classes hang on the walls. For those of you who get uptight in "modern (i.e., windowless) classrooms," this one has windows.

First Powell addressed the class and discussed the goals of the school. He stressed the importance of sharing information, not only from instructor to student, but from student to instructor and student to student. As a result, he said, knifemakers won't have to re-invent the wheel individually and very well may be able to advance the art to higher levels in, the future.

With the doors wide open on a beautifully sunny day, fires roar and smoke billows from the forges of the bladesmithing school. (Forbes photo)

end all students had completed a billet of Damascus steel, though there had been some failures when the steel got too hot or when welds didn't take. More was probably learned from the failures than from the successes. The Monday evening meal included of course knife talk.

Tuesday: Classroom discussion began with forge construction and timesaving tools that the knifemaker can make. The discussion also focused upon forge design and Damascus patterning. Bill demonstrated some of the knifemaking tools that he has made and discussed his views on the shaping of power hammer dies for the knifemaker.

We then went to the shop and, while some students made more Damascus steel billets, others completed Damascus blades. The predominate pattern throughout seemed to be maiden hair, respectively followed by the standard ocean and ladder patterns. Lunchtime found us talking knives and enjoying the Williams Tavern Restaurant. It was built in 1832, the nails in the floor still loose-and the food is excellent.

Tuesday afternoon two of us accepted the challenge of adjusting the Little Giant hammer. Much thought, more discussion, some trial and error, and success was ours. Those wishing to use the power hammer found the variables interesting and no complaints were heard (possibly due to the noise level of the power hammer).

The author (at left) and Bert Gaston cut a billet. Despite years of bladesmithing, the author learned a lot at the school. (Forbes photo)

The first morning classroom discussion emphasized the proper forge-welding temperature, maintenance of a coal fire, forge-welding procedures, and tips on the little things that cause failure.

We then went to the shop. All I can say is that it was beautiful. Six coal forges in a circle-a seventh side draft forge is in place and ready to use, surrounded by anvils, tongs and hammers. A 50-pound Little Giant power hammer sits in the center of the shop. Two walls are devoted to bench work space. On the bench are 2" x 72" belt grinders, vices, files and buffers. The school also has a metal cutting band saw, drill press, oxyacetylene torch, and electric arc welder. Both ends of the shop are graced with large doors for ventilation. The shop also has restroom facilities, running water, blackboard and office.

Making Damascus

We proceeded to coke some coal and make some Damascus billets, using a mixture of 01 and mild steel. At day's

The author (at left) gets a close-up view, as Bill Moran shows him how it's done. Note Moran's protective gear. (Forbes photo)

The students and their teacher, from left: Raymond Stofer, Scott Forbes, Kent Nicholson, Bert Gaston, Jerry Fisk, the author, Paul Inman and Bill Moran.

Instruction from Bill Moran

Wednesday: Classroom discussion was on survival knives. Moran brought some of his knives and he shared his views on the function and design of survival knives-not the double-edged kind you see advertised for survival in city streets but the large, well-balanced kind that can get you out of a bind or make life easier in the wilderness. Bill recommends a maximum weight of such knives at 1-1/2 pounds, blade lengths from 9 to 11 inches, and blades fully tapered to reduce weight and improve balance. Bill presented more of his forging techniques and theories on knife construction. Very little time was devoted to those esoteric features that do not relate to function and longevity.

Wednesday's shop time was spent with each student more or less doing his own thing under Moran's watchful eye. The problems that surfaced were all told to Bill and he usually had several alternative solutions, any of which would work, including "throw it away and start over." When you realize that "throw it away and start over" means carrying in and coaking another 100 pounds of coal, welding steel to a han-

dle, heating, fluxing, forge welding with a four-pound hammer, hammering the piece of steel to twice its original length, etc., you begin to realize the significance of those words!

Review of Knifemaker-Customer Relations

Wednesday evening found us cleaned up and eating catfish at one of Hope, Arkansas' fine restaurants. Many discussions focused on knifemaker-customer relations. For instance: A knifemaker can make an honest knife and still experience disappointment and failure with his customers. A knifemaker may suddenly find himself receiving a large volume of mail containing questions that need to be answered, checks and cash from people to whom he has never talked, and requests for knives that cannot be completed for years. Answering letters takes time—time that could be used making knives. Knives pay the bills and without cash, the deposits get spent and the knifemaker is in trouble.

Another pitfall comes when the knifemaker prices his knife. What is a fair price and how is it reached? Many great knifemakers are no longer making knives due to pricing that is too high or too low. Bill gives credit to his wife, Margaret.

for her support in all their endeavors. There are a lot of silent partners behind the successful knifemaker-his wife, family, friends and customers are the most prominent.

More Moran Blade Theory

Thursday: Classroom discussion consisted of a question-and-answer period, then Bill discussed handles. He stated that in his experience many old knives had been re-handled, some of them more than once; judging a knife by its handle can therefore be misleading. Moran then presented his methods of grinding forged blades. To quote Bill, "Anything with curves looks more lively than anything with flat angles." He presented more on the theory of the forged blade, discussing such concepts as grain flow, strength and toughness.

We then returned to the shop and the sweet smell of burning coals, ringing anvils and the sparks off the belt grinders. This was the day when some of the blades had taken their final polish and were etched in muriatic acid. The blade is placed in the acid and slowly but surely the pattern that has been designed by fire, hammer and file reveals itself.

Friday: Most of the day was spent in the shop, each student pursuing his own interests in the art of Damascus steel.

At day's end we swept the shop for the last time, closed the door and went to the classroom for our certificates.

The ABS School: A Summation

I have been making Damascus steel for four years. I learned the hard way through a lot of trial,error and phone calls. I took my first forging class under Moran five years ago and that week was the single largest influence upon the quality of my knives. Was this class worth it? I have to say yes. I wish that I could have taken the class years ago-it could have saved me months of lost labor. This was the first time I had even seen another knifemaker make layered Damascus steel. Bill's knowledge, methods and ability, coupled with his willingness to share, make for a top-notch learning opportunity..

Texarkana College, the Pioneer Washington Restoration Foundation and the ABS have put together a fine facility devoted to the preservation and development of an art that was facing extinction. I can honestly and unequivocably recommend the ABS school to anyone who is interested in making knives. The time and money you invest in the school can be the wisest investment that you can make in your knifemaking career.

The Great Blade Family

Properly instructed blade-making techniques, such as those practiced here by swordsmith Paul Champagne, are one way organizations benefit the great knife family.

There are many organizations in the world of knives, each contributing in its own way to provide a welcome place for its members. The leaders of the organizations have a tough job, receive little or no pay, and many times do the work of 10 for meager thanks. When all goes right not much is said, but when something goes wrong, they hear it all. Many times they find themselves caught between two factions, picking up the pieces and putting the organization together again. Each knife organization official deserves recognition and gratitude for the contributions he/she makes.

No cutlery organization, hereafter referred to collectively as organizations, has ever built a knife. Knives are made by people. All organizations can hope to do is encourage an environment that will, in whatever manner possible, nurture the creativity of their members.

I feel that individuals who join an organization in the hope that the organization will benefit them personally are not nearly as valuable to the organization as individuals who join with the intent of contributing to the common good. Both kinds of members require special attention from the leaders. The challenge is to identify and encourage their potential contribution to the organization as a whole. The other, and possibly greater, challenge is to keep the high achievers enthusiastic and within the scope of the organization.

The value of organizations to the individual members is significant. As a member of an organization, the individual may have much more influence on the world of knives than his efforts would were he standing alone.

Some controversy, while it may be uncomfortable for a time, is beneficial to organizations in that it provides the opportunity to learn and grow as the controversy is resolved. Organizations who openly address meaningful controversies take full advantage of the chance to advance and prosper. The ideal role of organizations is not to take sides, cry or laugh, but to understand.

All too often, however well intended at the start, organizations begin to promulgate rules that may not only detract from the value of the organizations, but, and more significantly, like rust to a blade, needlessly expend the energy of the leaders and make them old before their time. These kinds of issues can be avoided by a clear, definitive statement of purpose.

Without a clear and definite charter to govern his actions, each individual in the organization has his own conception as to the purpose of the organization and the degree of control it should assume over its members. I believe that the organization that rules least, and understands most, rules best.

Rules originally intended, for example, to preserve the integrity of the knives offered for sale by members may limit incoming members to certain qualifications that, while they may enhance the quality of the knives in the eyes of some, may also result in limiting the diversity and, therefore, potential contributions of the membership to the organization.

Some organizational problems, as well as opportunities, seem to develop in regard to the origin of the members themselves. Each brings to the organization his own vested interest. Should he be a knifemaker, knife collector or simply admire the art, due to human nature, his values are prominent in his mind whenever organizational decisions are made. This aspect of man is not all bad. Organizations that use the enthusiasm of the newcomer to strengthen their foundations will grow and all will prosper.

Another significant danger to any organization is that the leadership can be heavily influenced by a vocal minority that does not necessarily represent the majority, or speak to the betterment of the organization and knives as a whole. All need to have a voice but the message must be kept in perspective.

The history of man is filled with organizations, cultures and governments that have either ceased to exist or subjected their members to great stress and peril simply because their charters failed to address the basic nature of man. Tradition serves a purpose in all groups. However, when traditions become more important than the organization or its members and begin to mire the organization's growth and direction, it's time the traditions be judged on their own merits.

The First Lessons

When organizations teach, great care must be exercised in choosing the material to be presented. The first lessons learned will be most remembered by the new members. Therefore, if and when the new members should become the organizations' leaders, the lessons will come to represent the organizations' goals and direction. Instruction should instill knowledge, inspiration and a burning desire to seek more and explore where others have never been. Failure to exercise care in the lessons taught can lead to the establishment of traditions and dynasties that were never meant to exist in the first place. The greatest down side would be knowledge unshared and members lost.

Even America, supported by brilliant documents such as the Declaration of Independence, Constitution and Bill of Rights, finds its progress besieged by bureaucrats who hinder the individual solely for the benefit of their own empires. Empires that detract from the goals of the organization must have their feathers trimmed regularly or the organization surely will fail.

One area where I feel that organizations should exert all the influence possible is in the case of honesty. Should any member of a knife organization misrepresent his product to a customer, he should feel the total influence of that organization to make it right.

There's a desperate need for organizations in the world of knives. Properly designed organizations provide a home and welcome place for members, unity, purpose, comradeship and strength in numbers. Organizations can also assist members during the hard times and make the good times seem a little better. Many members will find themselves lost at one time or another and the brotherhood organizations provide is a welcome relief.

As individuals standing alone, knife enthusiasts have little voice in the effects of government upon the world of knives. The strength of the organization, however, grows with each new member. A ready example is the influence the National Rifle Association has on the challenge of gun control. The fact that knife enthusiasts face a similar challenge already has shown its ugly head in oppressive blade legislation and public schools that forbid knives rather than teach the more important lessons of responsibility, community and individual worth. It is hoped the recently formed American Knife & Tool Institute will become similar to the NRA's lobbying force in answering the challenge.

I had little choice in the selection of my first family but have come to live in the world of knives by choice. I met my wife and friends through blades, and I would have it no other way. I hope to contribute what I can and to watch the great knife family grow.

I'd like to express my thanks to the leaders of the organizations and to those who've given their time and abilities to make the world of cutlery better for everyone. Without organizations the world of knives would be little known, and many of its members would be isolated from the companionship they now enjoy.

ORIGINAL DATE OF ARTICLE PUBLICATION

TITLE:	PUBLICATION:	DATE:
52100 From A Metallurgist's View	BLADE	10/97
8 Keys For Modern Knifemakers	BLADE	01/96
A Knife For Mom	BLADE	06/93
A Knifemaker's Best Xmas Present	BLADE	02/93
A New Dress For Lady Knife	BLADE	08/91
A Special Knife For A Special Hand	BLADE	03/93
Avoid Knife Accidents: Here's How	BLADE	03&04/89
Best Military Knife Design Of All?	BLADE	02/96
Blades and Brothers	BLADE	10/96
Blades From Ball Bearings	BLADE	04/92
Can Your Knife Cut It?	BLADE	08/88
Caveman Cutler	BLADE	10/91
Copy	BLADE	12/96
Curves	BLADE	06/96
Dick And Dorothy Iiams: Thanks For The Good Times	BLADE	09/97
Ed Ties The Knot	BLADE	05/96
Find The Most Solid Ground For Your Blade	BLADE	01&02/89
Follow-Up: Freeze Treating 5160	BLADE	07/95
Forging The Fowler Way		
Part 1 The Trick Is To Forge It Thick	BLADE	04/97
Part 2 Elements Of Basic Forging	BLADE	05/97
Part 3 How To Forge A Blade	BLADE	06/97
Part 4 Normalizing & Annealing	BLADE	07/97
Good Knives & Good Sheaths-A Perfect Fit	BLADE	09&10/88
Hammered and Forged: ABS School	BLADE	05&06/89
Heroes	BLADE	07/96
How To Freeze Quench Your Steel	BLADE	06/95
How To Heat Treat: The Spirit Of The Forged Blade	BLADE	06/92
How To Tell The Good Information From The Bad	BLADE	04/95
How You Can Ensure The Future Of Knives	BLADE	03/94
If It's Not A Folder, Is It Fixed?	BLADE	12/95
Just Use Your Imagination	BLADE	07&08/94
Knives Tell Stories	BLADE	09/95
Knife Or Death	BLADE	09/92
Knifesharpenophobia	BLADE	12/91
Knives In School	BLADE	01/97
Multiple Quenching	KNIVES ILLUSTRATED	Spring 1991
Mystery Of The D-Guard Bowie	BLADE	11/96
Pass The Billets Please	BLADE	09/93
Reflections On Steel	BLADE	03/95
Relive The Past With Bronzed Blades	BLADE	12/88
Seduced By The Iron Mistress	BLADE	12/94
Snake Steak	BLADE	08/93
Solved: The D-Guard Bowie Mystery	BLADE	02/97
Sweet Dreams of Steel	BLADE	10/95
Tales From The Forge	BLADE	03/96
Thanks, Pilgrims!	BLADE	01/97
That First Knife	BLADE	09/97
The Back Of The Blade	BLADE	02/92

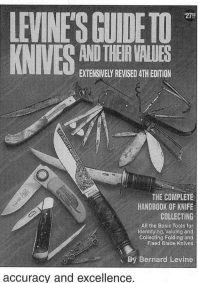